C000253667

Advance praise for

# My Ackee Tree

"Any good cook knows that layering one's seasonings is necessary to make a great dish, but in *My Ackee Tree*, Suzanne Barr shows how layers also make a life rich, full, and complex. Through the recounted conversations, meals, and recipes that thread together her upbringing, Suzanne brings food to life, and life to food. Communicating an inspiring and quintessentially Black experience of finding oneself on life's winding, rocky, joyful, not-so-straightforward road, her stories will ignite scent memories for anyone with roots in the Caribbean, and her recipes, when you cook them, will foster a love of that same world, no matter where you're from."
—David Zilber, *New York Times* bestselling co-author of *The Noma Guide to Fermentation*

"Suzanne Barr is not only a brilliant chef but she's also a talented, honest storyteller. In *My Ackee Tree*, she shares her amazing story, her love of food, music, family, adventure, and her journey to become a chef, wife, and mother. Her generous heart and soul is poured out on every page with passion, emotion, humor, strength, and resilience. *My Ackee Tree* is inspiring and heartwarming—and such a gift."
—Chef Lynn Crawford, bestselling author of *Farm to Chef* and *Hearth & Home*

"Part love letter, part coming-of-age tale, Suzanne Barr's stories in *My Ackee Tree* build a tapestry of will and hope. Driven by love for her mother, Barr is able to fulfill a promise to herself: she cares for her dying mother and discovers the gift of her native food. This is her personal homecoming. It nurtures her soul and spirit, and it's where she discovers her passion to be a chef. Bravo!"
—Alexander Smalls, author of *Meals, Music, and Muses* and *Between Harlem and Heaven*

"I loved Suzanne's memoir. It is a delightful mix of family, food, and love. It seems cliché to say it, but I really wish I could be one of her regulars, enjoying her signature dish of Big Chick Thighs and feeling the magic she and her husband Johnnie transmit to their diners."
—Kristina Gill, food editor and co-author of *Tasting Rome*

"To a fellow chef, Suzanne has always been an inspiration. Learning more about her story, and all her triumphs and all her trials, only inspires me more. Thoughtfully written and with delicious recipes, it's a must-read."
—Amanda Cohen, co-author of *Dirt Candy*

"I was instantly taken by Suzanne's good nature and her authenticity. Her cooking is all about robust flavors with a personal twist, but it's always solidly rooted in her family background. We've only had a small taste of what Suzanne is capable of in the kitchen and I look forward to watching that evolution."
—Mark McEwan, author of *Great Food at Home* and *Mark McEwan Rustic Italian*

"The strength and power of women in kitchens not only rests in our dedication to our craft, but in our stories and in our deep connections with our past and each other. Suzanne Barr has given us a beautiful glimpse into this strength, where we learn about how she built an inspiring career on the foundation of family and community. She is one of the most important voices in food today, not only because of what sets her apart, but because of how—through her skill and dedication, her sincerely caring and rich heart—she pulls us all together."
—Lisa Donovan, author of *Our Lady of Perpetual Hunger*

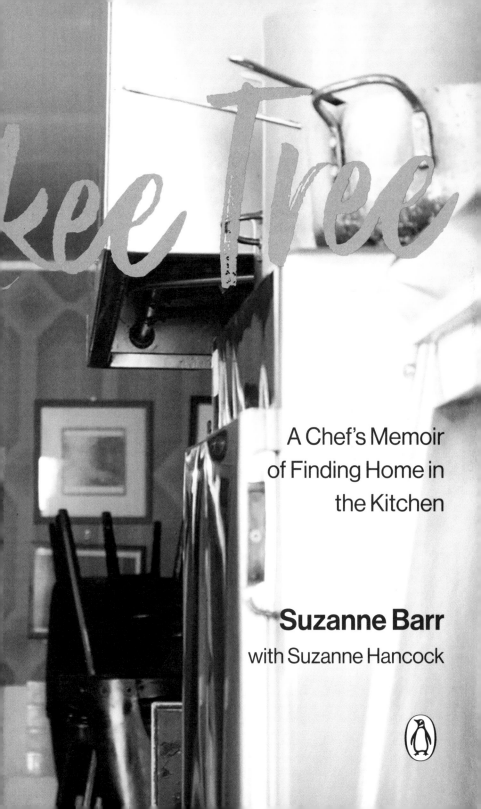

A Chef's Memoir
of Finding Home in
the Kitchen

**Suzanne Barr**

with Suzanne Hancock

PENGUIN

an imprint of Penguin Canada, a division of Penguin Random House Canada Limited

Canada · USA · UK · Ireland · Australia · New Zealand · India · South Africa · China

First published 2022

www.penguinrandomhouse.ca

Library and Archives Canada Cataloguing in Publication

Title: My ackee tree: a chef's memoir of finding home in the kitchen / Suzanne Barr with
Suzanne Hancock.
Names: Barr, Suzanne (Cook), author. | Hancock, Suzanne, 1971- author.
Identifiers: Canadiana (print) 20210220791 | Canadiana (ebook) 20210220988 |
ISBN 9780735239500 (hardcover) | ISBN 9780735239517 (EPUB)
Subjects: LCSH: Barr, Suzanne (Cook) | LCSH: Cooks—Canada—Biography. |
LCSH: Women cooks—Canada—Biography. | CSH: Jamaican Canadians—Biography. |
LCGFT: Autobiographies.
Classification: LCC TX649.B37 A3 2022 | DDC 641.5092—dc23

Book design by Terri Nimmo
Cover design by Terri Nimmo
Cover photography by Samuel Engelking
Cover illustrations by Kamoy Nicola Williams
Photography on pages ii–iii, 47, 86, 118, 135, 143, 220–21 by Suzanne Robertson,
Photography on pages x–xi, xii–xiii, 94–95, 156–57, 188, 196, 200–1, 214–15, and 222
by Samuel Engelking, Illustrations on pages 9, 117, 159, and 230 by Kamoy Nicola Williams,
Photography on page 32 by Sid Grant, Photography on page 151 by Bettina Bogar,
Rite of Passage Menu on page 178 provided care of The Gladstone Hotel and created
for its Chef in Residence Program created and curated by Christina Zeidler
All other interior images were provided courtesy of the author

Printed in the United States of America

1st Printing

Penguin
Random House
PENGUIN CANADA

*For my grandparents and my great-grandparents.*
*And for Nicey and Sonny.*

# AUTHOR'S NOTE

## by Suzanne Barr

Dear readers, please understand that names of some of the subjects have been changed to protect their identity.

Some of the stories shared are from a direct source, as I was able to interview certain people. I wanted their voices to be heard in the book. The rest reflects my memory of events.

If certain names and specific dates are not mentioned, it was our intention to keep the narrative moving and to focus on the larger story.

It is an honour and a gift to have the opportunity to share my story unapologetically. And to allow the smells, laughter, recipes, and memories to tell my truths.

# PROLOGUE

My truck is full of thirty-five-dollar used chairs from an Italian restaurant on College Street that's getting a facelift. I'm on my way to the dry cleaner where I'm supposed to pick up a whole whack of napkins that the seamstress was making from a ream of denim that I'd found a few months before. The seamstress doesn't have them all ready, although we'd agreed on a date weeks before, and I'm pissed. I think we'll have enough for the evening, though, so I get back in the truck and call Johnnie, who's at the restaurant patching and painting some spots we missed. It's opening night. Our restaurant, Saturday Dinette, with its whitewashed walls and black trim, with its black-and-white tile and elegant countertop is about to open its doors. Johnnie tells me that it's no big deal, we'll have enough napkins, come home. And the restaurant really does feel like home. We've been working non-stop for three months to turn it into our dream restaurant, and we've spent way more time there than at our studio loft a few blocks away. He's right, it's no big deal, and I choose to let the frustration escape through the window and disappear along the Gardiner Expressway.

I'm listening to the De La Soul song, "A Roller Skating Jam Named 'Saturdays,'" the inspiration for the name of our restaurant. And "Dinette" (definition: a dining alcove or nook) because we want it to be a small, family-style place where people can come for modern comfort food. A diner, with all the history that diners have represented since the era of sit-ins and the civil rights movement. It's 4 o'clock, and doors open at 7, so I'll have lots of time to put the finishing touches on the bites we are going to offer: Rosemary Socca, Zucchini Latkes, Sticky Ribs. We've sent invitations out to friends, family, and neighbours who've been watching us renovate for months, and we're hoping for some walk-ins, too. Sitting at the red light, waiting to turn left onto Carlaw, my phone rings.

"Hey, Dr. Harris."

"Hi, there. I have the results from the blood work we did last week."

I'd been feeling a little light-headed and not quite myself, and they were testing my thyroid function, iron levels, and, also, for pregnancy.

"It looks like you're pregnant, Suzanne."

Green light and tears. So many tears. I can't stop crying. And I'm not crying for joy; I'm crying because I can't do this. I can't be pregnant. I don't want to be pregnant. I'm about to open my very first restaurant, and I can't do that and have a baby at the same time. I should pull over, but I can't think. Along Dundas, everything comes at me in waves—missing my mum, meeting Johnnie in France, moving to Canada while longing to be back in Brooklyn, finding a space on the corner of Gerrard Street East and Logan Avenue that felt like the perfect place to open a restaurant. And then that final, sickening wave that threatens to drown me: Will I be a good mother?

Our catering company, Pepper and Sprout, is how we pay the bills right now, and it takes up all of our daylight hours. At night, we renovate the Dinette. It's exhausting and beyond stressful, but it's exciting like nothing ever has been before. This is going to be my restaurant, and I'm going to knock it out of the park. I've always been a self-starter—a daughter of hard-working immigrants, I throw myself wholeheartedly into everything I do. Late nights after working on the floors, or cleaning the walls, or setting the place up, I can already feel Saturday Dinette as a busy place, music blaring, frying pans smoking, orders for our special brand of comfort food flying out of the ticket machine.

I pull up beside the restaurant and sit in the car for a little while, taking deep breaths and cleaning up my smeared mascara. I think of my mother, who had her first baby when she was eighteen and was pressured to marry the father. I wonder how profoundly alone she felt. I feel her and her great strength, and I savour the moment of deep communion. At the same time, I wonder if this pregnancy will break me. I don't know many people in Toronto. My sister, Tanya, lives across the continent in Los Angeles, my dad is in Plantation, Florida, where I grew up, and Amanda and Maria, my best friends, are in Florida, as well. I suddenly feel totally alone. It's a feeling that I'm used to, and that comes naturally, and it's a feeling that I'm trying to overcome.

Home has always been hard to define. Is it Florida, where I grew up? Is it Toronto, where I was born? Or does it stretch further back than that? Is it land that I barely know, land where my ancestors lived in Jamaica? Is it in my memories of my mother?

Johnnie and some of the young women who work for us at Pepper and Sprout, and who will become the backbone of the Dinette, come out to the car, and he taps the trunk for me to open it. There's excitement about the chairs and a general buzz of anticipation about the evening. Johnnie realizes that I'm not getting out of the car and hops into the front seat.

"Are you okay?"

"Yeah, but I'm pissed about the napkins. I wish I knew another seamstress. And Dr. Harris called to say that I'm pregnant."

"Wait. What?"

And then the tears come again and I tell him that I feel so alone and that I can't have a baby, we're about to open a restaurant.

His arms feel good, and he says, "You're not alone. I'm here. We can do this together. I agree, it's not the best time, but, holy shit, we're going to have a baby!" He's crying too. I've only known Johnnie for a year, and we're about to become business partners as well as parents. I look at him, and I realize that I'm not alone. Maybe we can do this. We have to do this.

We gather the staff together and say, "Let's get this restaurant open."

# ONE

# CHILDHOOD

Nah every crab hole get crab

I don't like sitting still, and music is my medicine, my constant inspiration. I see flavours and smell colours and want my dishes to be music, to do to bellies what the tunes do to my soul. I'm Canadian, Jamaican, African, Indigenous, naturalized American, with deep ties to the UK, under everything to the earth and seas where I find my flavours. Here I am setting down who I am, and sometimes I'm not sure. I've been a photographer, a stylist, an activist, a producer at MTV, a private chef in the Hamptons, a judge of cooking shows, a student, and a mentor. I've drunk wine in a crater created by a meteor and seen the darkness and light of childbirth. I've lost family, gained family, owned a beautiful restaurant, and someone once paid me one hundred thousand dollars for a bowl of curry chicken. What I know is that I keep wanting to surprise my tongue. To put flavours together that take me to all those places I've never been and make me look anew at the places I remember.

I'm not sitting still. I can't sit still. I'm all over the map in my head, in my memories, and I wish I had more time in the day. I wish I could put these words on a plate for you.

Cooking is my love. I wake up, walk, think, and dance as a cook. Food brings people together. It brings me to you. I fight for justice and equality, and I know that the best way to make people feel better is to feed them good food. The best way to make friends is to sit down at the table.

That's how I'm thinking of this book. I'll go through the cupboards and get some facts. Facts like ingredients. Born here, grew there, studied for these years there, and loved, and loved by so-and-so. And the ingredients become this dish. Me. My life.

I'll put some music on. Some dancehall. Some soul. Talk to Mummy and Auntie and all the Nevilles we knew. Sing through the hard times. Play some nineties alternative rock and dance with my brilliant sister while I cook.

Here are some ingredients.

I grew up in a place called Plantation, Florida.

And it wasn't until starting at the School of Visual Arts New York City, and I had to answer the question "Where are you from?" that I realized saying "Plantation, Florida," was fucked up. People's eyes widened. "Really? There's a place called Plantation?" Yep. Forty minutes from Miami, safe and suburban, the place where my parents bought land when we moved to the United States from Canada. It was affordable and up-and-coming, and the name didn't seem to bother my Jamaican-born parents.

We were one of the first Black families to own and develop on 27th Court. We were the immigrants who moved to the neighbourhood with our fruit trees and attention to detail. A pride in ownership. My mum, Eunice Adassa Facey, designed our house from floor to ceiling. The house of her dreams. Modern, open concept, with high vaulted ceilings and lots of skylights. The outside of the house was grey, and the facade was enlivened by my mum's prized roses. There was a waterfall, and a pebble garden that my dad cared for religiously.

*Plantation*. When you say something enough, it kind of loses its power. Plantation was a real place with strip malls and a movie theatre; it was my friends' houses and palm trees and blue sky. The official motto of the town is "The grass is greener."

It's impossible to separate the name of the town I grew up in from the Antebellum South, an era of economic growth in the United States that was built entirely on the backs of Black slaves. Plantations were places where enslaved people were raped and died. They were places where culture was beaten out of people, where sexuality was destroyed, places where white supremacy reigned. And the legacy of slavery is still so intimately tied to our modern-day culture. Inequities in wealth and injustices in policing continue to disproportionately affect Black communities, and their causes are deeply rooted in slavery.

When my parents moved to Plantation, less than 5 percent of the population was Black.

What they wanted, and what they built, was a safe home for our family. And family can be complicated. My mum, Eunice, and my dad, George, had two kids together: my older sister, Tanya, and me. But I have five other siblings, and some I know better than others. By the time my parents arrived in Plantation, they wanted to settle in and to build a place where we could dream our own dreams. I still wince a little when I tell people I'm going home to see my dad in Plantation, but that little suburb with the appalling name is where my own strength was built, and it is the place where my love of food originated.

*I'm in a red bowl being held by my mother.*
*I am tamarind paste.*
*Coconut. Allspice.*
*Bay leaves. Callaloo.*
*Saltfish. Plantains. Curry.*
*Her legendary apple pie.*

The old Dutch oven sits on the stove, full of bush tea. In another pot, day-old provisions wait to be stored in the fridge. Provisions are those starchy side dishes that often accompany Caribbean dishes. Mummy liked to combine green banana, boiled dumpling, and yam. Add a Scotch bonnet pepper, thyme, garlic, and salt. Classic. Delicious.

"Tanya and Suzanne, come make salad," Mummy yells.

She says it in a loving tone, with a slight British Jamaican accent.

"Coming, Mummy," we call back.

We definitely embraced American foods in my childhood kitchen, but Jamaican ingredients were key. My family didn't travel back to Jamaica often, but food was central in keeping us connected to our roots. Our weekly menu featured things like rice and gungo peas with a side of meat lasagna, or curried goat with apple pie. Jamaican dishes were always present in our house.

Mummy's in the kitchen in a blue T-shirt and black above-the-knee shorts, and her voice carries through the house like a megaphone. She isn't a singer. But if you're in the backyard, or front yard, the alto range and bass undertones interrupt the flow of whatever you're doing. We're needed.

"Tanya . . . Tanya . . . ," I yell. "Mummy, Tanya's not coming to help."

My weapon. A swift nudge to my back and sometimes a pinch.

"Ouch," I scream. "Mummy, Tanya hit me."

"Mummy, I didn't touch her."

A big sister who knew her calling wasn't in the kitchen, but when Mummy called, you answered.

"Girls, wash your hands!"

Tanya motions for us to meet at the kitchen sink. We push each other to get to the soap first and then race to tea towels hanging on the oven door.

"Stop horsing around, you two."

Always salad with dinner. Usually iceberg lettuce, but sometimes romaine. Gently tearing the leaves, glaring at Tanya. Eventually a smile on both our mouths.

Mummy is what we called her. She wasn't *Mom*. She wasn't *Mommy*. She was *Mum*. That's the British influence. It stuck.

Mummy had rhythm. Her swift moves in the kitchen were noted. Gliding on the off-white tiles from stovetop to counter. Marvin Gaye coming from the speaker, she sings along and moves her hips from side to side as she washes the chicken with vinegar. She was five foot six, slim, not too tall, not skinny, not fat. She loved to walk. But she *loved* to dance.

The kitchen is warm and full of scents: curry, allspice, vinegar, fried dumplings, fried fish. Backsplash speckled with oil, greasy laminate countertop. The sink contains Mummy's teacup, spoons, lunch plates, and a red plastic bowl. The bowl was her main tool. It was faded and had burn marks from the dishwasher. She used it for everything. Inside was tinged yellow from spices, the yellow rubbing off on everything she made.

Like the omnipresent smell of curry, there was always a reused jar or cup on the counter that would hold "good" oil—leftover oil that was used for frying plantains or dumplings, or oil skimmed off the top of some fatty meat dish. My mother did things in the kitchen that she must have seen her mother and grandmother do when she was just a child. Maybe she never formally understood how those traditions (like holding on to the oil) deepened the flavour of her food, but she never forgot them, and through her life they were part of her cooking.

That kitchen in Florida. It was open and airy, with lots of space for meal preparation. Sunday dinners were important and meant all-day prep that ended with three courses served in the dining room on the white eyelet tablecloth. A mess at the end that my sister, mum, and I would clean up while Daddy watched a game in the other room. There were spice jars lined up against the wall. Containers for tea, sugar, cornmeal, and flour. A black-and-white speckled countertop connected the kitchen and the family room with two tall stools where we used to perch.

Tanya and I race each other and plop down on the stools. She spins right, I spin left.

"Mummy, who's a better dancer? Tanya or me?"

She looks at us with her signature stare—we know not to push it further—and she smiles.

My parents didn't make a conscious effort to teach me how to cook. They were just cooking all the time, and I was there watching.

Staring at my mother's hands around that bowl.

The sky was always blue in Florida. Royal, sapphire, Egyptian, olympic, electric. Tanya and I wanted seasons, to watch leaves fall in autumn and wear snow boots in winter. We sometimes shuffled through family photos of a life before, memories of winters in Toronto with our cousins before we moved to Florida. But the view out my window in Plantation was pretty constant. Blue from the sky and green from a tree that never changed.

The tree, though, was something special: ackee. Jamaica's national fruit. The poor thing rarely fruited, but it was still like a Jamaican flag in front of our house.

Of all the jobs Mummy asked me to do in the kitchen, cleaning ackee was my favourite.

Returning home from a Caribbean market, Daddy places a whole sack of ackee on the table. Bright-red fruit peeks from the bag. Each pod is the size of Mummy's palm, and they look like beautiful under-sea flowers, opening.

Tanya and I stand beside her at the counter.

"Don't mash up de ackee."

We roll our eyes. "We know, we know. You tell us every time."

She sucks air through her teeth from behind pursed lips, then lets out a short, sharp kiss. It's a technique my mum mastered before my time. Jamaicans are experts at kissing teeth.

A short kiss means minor irritation. A longer, deeper kiss means that Mummy is vexed. Kissing teeth can indicate annoyance, anger, and even joy . . .

It's only a short kiss this time, and Mummy is showing us that she disapproves of our eye-rolling and our sass.

"Put the seeds here in this bowl."

Her accent was subtle, but Jamaican Patois would shine when she was vexed, or when she was reminiscing with one of her friends. "Cha" (no, man) was one of her staples.

"Cha, cant bada with de childe, pickney de too facety."

Mummy had an arsenal of dialects and accents for everyday use.

I didn't love the actual work of cleaning ackee—gently separating the fleshy parts of the fruit from the shiny black seeds—but I *loved* knowing that we'd have ackee and saltfish the next morning. Ackee has a mild flavour, kind of nutty, and a buttery texture that pairs perfectly with salted fish.

"This one isn't open, Mummy."

She grabs it out of my hand.

"It's poisonous. The fumes will kill you," she says.

It always shocked me, that fact. If it's eaten too soon, before it opens on its own, it can be toxic.

She sifts through the bag, pulling out any closed pods, and places them on the marble windowsill above the sink. It's where she puts tea bags she's only used once, the kitchen sponge, her beloved spider plant.

Ackee flesh gets under my nails. It's kind of slimy but not gooey. Firm yet soft to touch.

"It looks like a brain!" Tanya and I giggle.

"Cheeky innit! Stop playing with the food and finish up," Mummy says firmly.

A seven-pound bag of ackee turns into one pound of flesh. Shells go in the garbage, black seeds are sprinkled in the backyard in hopes of another tree.

Cooking salt cod is a process. Mummy soaks the fish overnight in water, and then drains it the next day. She adds fresh water and brings it to a boil. The water spills over, and she kisses her teeth; she drains the water, boils it again, drains again, boils it for a third time, and drains it once more. Each time she changes the water, more salt is pulled from the fish.

When the fish is ready, she parboils the ackee flesh. Then she flakes the fish into big, succulent chunks and adds crispy sliced bacon, tomatoes, thyme, and scallions. Cooked ackee looks like scrambled eggs with its firm fluffiness and light-yellow hue.

There's power and deep memories in that combination of flavours for me, and that's why I rarely cook ackee and saltfish myself. It sits too heavy on my heart. All I think about with that dish is my mum.

Here is the briefest timeline:

My mother grew up in Saint Elizabeth Parish, Jamaica—approximately 125 kilometres west of the capital, Kingston—until she was twelve years old.

At twelve, she immigrated to London, England, where her father had moved in search of work on the railroads.

At eighteen she had a son, Wayne, and was sent by her family, without Wayne, to Canada.

In Toronto, she met my dad, George.

Sometimes people called my mum Nicey and my dad Sonny. Nicknames, "yard names," are common in Jamaican culture. And sometimes that name sticks. What's your Christian name, again? No one remembers.

Nicey and Sonny in Toronto trying to figure it out.

My sister, Tanya, and I were born there.

And when I was four, and Tanya six, my parents moved to Florida.

"Suzanne, come here, go set the table—dinner ready soon."

That countertop between the kitchen and the living room was like a stage. It was where so many conversations happened.

I'm ten, Tanya's twelve, and we're spinning on those chairs. Hold on tight.

My parents tell us about Headley, my dad's son who he hadn't seen in years. He was out of my dad's life, and their connection had been broken. He lived in Toronto, and through a mutual friend, they had found each other again.

I'm overjoyed, but confused.

"How could you keep this a secret?"

"What does he look like?"

"Is he tall?"

"Will he come live with us?"

My family is tangled and full of secrets. Stories left unspoken and unheard. Whole chapters in my parents' lives are buried under so much baggage they never see the light. *Nothing to see here, nothing at all, keep walking, keep moving.* Still, some stories were revealed to us, and many were told as we sat on those stools, in that space between.

"What happened to Wayne?"

"I have a pain in my back."

"We should send her to a crazy house."

"Mummy's sick."

"Get out of my house."

Mummy rarely sat on the stools. She always stood in the kitchen while having a snack, drinking her tea, talking to friends on the phone. Mummy smiled through the stories and the revelations, but you could see she was bottling things up. Some people blamed her for breaking up my dad's past relationships. Tanya and I protected her fiercely. She was love. Beauty. So many admirers. She always wanted to make people laugh, and she was playful. Nicey was Star as they say in Jamaica. A country girl with a fearless passion, maybe a bit naive.

I was home in Florida a couple of years ago looking at a framed photo of my parents' wedding day when a picture behind that photo fell to the floor. It was Mummy as a teenager, sitting on a bed, surrounded by wedding presents. Her eyes were hollow, stunned. She looked defeated and scared. Nothing like the picture of a joyful bride.

In my wedding pictures, I'm beaming. I'm happy. I'm in love. Staring at that photo of my mum, I'm lost in that moment with her. Maybe we're all a little frightened of our future.

I thought about the fact that she didn't tell many detailed stories of her past, of England and Jamaica, and almost everything that I've learned about her is from her siblings and her friends. Like many people, I'm sure, I'd do anything to be able to go back in time, to any day before she died, maybe one of the afternoons we spent just south of Fort Lauderdale on Dania Beach, so I could ask her questions. I'd ask her about Jamaica, about her mother and her grandmother, about what it felt like to travel from sun-drenched Saint Elizabeth to the grey streets of London. Did she listen to ska or dancehall to make those streets less grey? I'd ask her about her life before she had kids. I would listen to the voice that was silenced so many years ago. Did she have anything to tell me? How should I face my own challenges? So many questions toppling over each other. They fall like glass hitting the floor. Shattering quickly. Missing pieces in the corners lost forever until you go searching and they cut you.

You can tell me anything.

But that's not how it works.

"Stop spinning in the chairs! You're too heavy; they're going to break," she yells. The chairs eventually bend forward and lose their spinning power. My dad replaces them with dark wood chairs, embellished with metal grommets. These would never spin.

My father doesn't like memory lane either. His young life in Kingston was tough—those memories aren't discussed without much prodding, and the answers always leave me wanting more. I get it. Why dwell on a past full of confrontation and hurt when you've spent your whole life trying to escape it?

From a young age, my dad helped his mother, Francis Hilton, sell food at markets in Kingston. They sold yams, bananas, curry chicken, dumplings, and a collection of other prepared meals. Daddy would have to get up before the sun to help his mother cook, then transport the food to the markets, then back home to do it all over again. I see his hands, pruney from washing pots, pans, plates, and serving utensils. His bare feet throbbing from hours of standing. His shoulders locked in position, close to his ears—the stress stays there. Sleepless nights as the routine played over and over in his mind. This is true of many chefs. But he was a boy. Dreaming of playing in the sand on the beach. Riding on the handlebars of his father's bike.

My dad is an incredible cook. He's intuitive and creative and my friends in Plantation would fight to come to our house for some of my dad's stewed peas and rice or curry goat. But when I ask him if he liked cooking when he was a kid, he says he didn't think of it as cooking—not in the sense of sharing food and giving pleasure, but as simply a job to be done.

He and his mother, working together. Peeling the yams, butchering chickens, lugging meals through busy streets with the cars and the diesel, and doing it day after day. A different idea of family cooking.

My dad had a difficult relationship with his father, which was never resolved. I can see that so clearly now. He usually chooses not to show his emotions. He's a bit numb.

My grandfather was a handyman who did odd jobs all over Kingston. I don't know much about him (I've never even seen a photo, and it's hard getting my dad to talk about him), but I do know that he died in a biking accident on his way home from work when my dad was fourteen years old. Life got harder for my grandmother after her husband's death, and feeding all those mouths became impossible. My dad did other work to help pay the bills, and his mother remarried a short time after my grandfather died. My father must have felt betrayed. He was the man of the house, and here was someone to replace him. There was probably some tension between Daddy and his new stepfather, and his home became a place that didn't feel safe.

I'm sure he didn't understand the hurt his mother experienced after losing her husband. Her longing for a man to help raise their family. Her loss. Her trauma. Their trauma. It never leaves, it just gets suppressed, hidden, passed on.

My dad's anger lay dormant in those old wounds.

The house became more crowded, and soon there was no room for my dad, who went to live in a rooming house.

The only place that brought Daddy some solace was North Street Congregational Church, run by a minister named Mr. Mackie. The church became his home, and the congregation his family. He was alone but lifted by the will and hope of faith. I imagine it gave him the ability to believe that his life was worth more. He would have to forgive and forget the past to set a course for the future.

In 1965, a church connection helped my dad move to the Bahamas where he got a job as a bartender on a cruise ship. The ship eventually made its way to Miami, and when it docked, my dad found the Canadian embassy, where he applied for a visa. He had a friend who lived in Toronto, and he thought he'd try his luck in Canada.

When I imagine walking in his shoes, I'm stunned by his fearlessness. Alone, he trekked forward and he never looked back. He made his way to the corner of Bloor Street West and Bathurst Street, right near Honest Ed's department store, where there were affordable rooming houses and many Jamaican immigrants. Honest Ed's closed in 2016 and was demolished the following year. It was a landmark, a beacon, for those early Caribbean settlers who came to Toronto. And the area around the store became their neighbourhood and felt like their "yard." I often pass through that neighbourhood and have visions of a young George trudging through the snowy streets to catch the bus or jump on the subway. Winters were brutal for him. Minus thirty and snow as high as cars. The tastes of home sometimes impossible to find. But that block was the centre of his new world. He wanted it all and he was hungry. My father is a fighter. He's charismatic and funny, crafty and street smart. He would tell me that he was a ladies' man. Sonny Bwoy. A smooth talker. He could persuade and get what he needed. He laughs when he shares the memories of how much women loved Sonny Bwoy. "I was hot. Ladies couldn't leave me alone. It was the sixties, man."

He knew how hard life could be because of his experience as a kid, but he didn't allow that to remain his truth. The visions and lessons he learned from pastor Mackie kept running through his mind. He used his natural talents, his wit, his desires. And ultimately, his faith. He found his friend and he made others, but what a dramatic change in environment.

If I can exhibit even half of his strength throughout my life, I'll be proud.

I'm sitting on the counter watching Mummy wash the carefully selected Granny Smith apples for her legendary Dutch Apple Pie. Then she peels them. She starts from the top of the apple and removes the skin like an expert swordswoman exposing the juicy flesh. She never cuts herself, and she never needs a cutting board. Claw grip is for amateurs. We slice and boil the apples, combine the flour and sugar and spices, and then we pour the filling into a Keebler pie crust, and the flour mixture goes on top. The mound of the pie is embedded with her fingerprints as she firmly but ever so gently locks in the flavours of cinnamon, allspice, and nutmeg. She takes my hands and presses them into the pie topping. Her soft hands on top of mine.

The schools in Plantation had funding and good reputations, another reason my parents built there. They wanted us to study hard and expected us to enjoy the advantages they felt they hadn't had: do the right thing, be good citizens. It meant following rules.

I went to Nova High School, a magnet school designed to attract a diverse student body from throughout the area. There were rich kids and poor kids. I was right in the middle. Nova was known for its multiculturalism and diversity, but it was in Davie, which had its own history with racism. Historically, it was a Southern, rural, Confederate flag–flying, good-old-boy town. Once you were through the gates of the school, though, it was a multicultural mecca. People from Sierra Leone, Venezuela, Thailand, all over the world.

My parents didn't want me to be Jamaican—they didn't want us to speak Patois in the house and said, *You're Canadian, not Jamaican*. Looking back, I think that only made me want to learn more about Jamaica—anything you deny your child will hold a greater interest.

My mum told me just enough about my great-grandmother, that she was a Maroon—a descendant of African slaves who escaped and then established free communities in the mountains. It made me proud, curious. Who was that woman? What were her stories?

My parents never wanted to go back to visit. As a teenager, I only took one very short trip to Jamaica with my mum and Tanya to visit our cousins. They lived in the hills on the outskirts of Kingston with a breathtaking view of the city and the ocean. I got a sense of their neighbourhood and a little of the city—I remember a food market and a day at the beach—but we stayed close to their house. When we did drive through the city, I thought about my dad as a kid running through those streets.

Jamaica made my parents who they were. Resilient, hard-working, slightly aloof, generous, fun-loving (and good cooks!). What did they carry in their hearts from home?

The other role Jamaica played was at a deep subconscious level—one I didn't understand for a long time. For all my years in that Plantation kitchen, I was literally eating the country, the flavours that made my parents. If I noticed the importance of this on my identity, I underestimated it.

Canada was a country, not an identifiable culture. It was where the rest of my extended family lived. Black American history didn't feel like my own. The culture, the food, the traditions. I didn't know much then. Fitting in was all I could do. When I was with the Black kids at school, I wanted to be Blacker. When I was with white kids, I wanted to be whiter. I got pushback from the Black kids sometimes because I dressed too white, but I could never seem to be Black enough, either.

Initially, kids didn't know what to make of me. How could a Black girl be from Canada?

"You sound like a white girl!"

"What kind of accent is that? You don't sound American!"

My mother had an accent, not me. My father had an accent, not me.

"You don't sound like a Black girl," they said.

My dad had a job at a big printing company and, for extra money, my mum cleaned the company's office. She did the bathrooms and vacuumed the floors on Sunday nights after dinner. Sometimes she brought me and Tanya. Was I old enough to realize she was making sacrifices for us? I remember when Z Cavaricci jeans were popular, Mummy used her extra money to buy a pair for Tanya and me to share.

Hard work was central to my parents' identities, but they also needed to unwind sometimes. They threw some legendary parties.

I see us now spending hours getting ready for the guests, Mummy's friend Myrna from Canada and Uncle Fitzy, Phyllis, Lloyd, and always a Neville. Neighbourhood friends and faces I kind of recognize but can't name.

Mop the kitchen floor. Vacuum every inch of carpet so the vacuum marks are perfectly aligned. Polish the dining table using Pledge. Move the couch and corner chair to make room for a dance floor.

And cook.

Mummy mixes macaroni salad in the red bowl, jerk marinated chicken wings roasting in the oven, meatballs hand-rolled with just the right amount of spice, rice and peas fluffed in a pot.

Daddy sets up the bar: Johnnie Black, overproof rum, an oversized bottle of vodka. He fills the fridge with Heinekens and Red Stripe. The food is served in the kitchen and the main dining room is out of bounds because the carpet is too pristine to walk on. The kitchen is always open.

My dad's friend Earl brings crates of records through the door. He's the DJ. I'm standing too close, maybe, but I love watching him set up. He's sifting through Daddy's collection, countless forty-fives and twelve-inches: Exodus, Sweetness, Cliff Hanger. Records go here organized by genre and release date. Jacket goes here on the back of the chair. Favourite forty-fives close to the decks. Food plate here. Beer sweats here. Earl is short, dark-skinned, and his face shows a life lived. The whites of his eyes the colour of sunrise. He's a wizard.

Once he's set up, our bodies start shaking from his magic. The party's going. Earl reads the room and paces the night, saves the big tunes for after the dishes are done. Buju Banton, Maxi Priest, Peter Tosh, Beres Hammond, Smokey Robinson.

Watch this, Beres!

Hear why!

Slow beat and bass comes in soft, and everyone in the room, kids and all, wining and skanking and riding a train or the slide, see her hips, to some place where you can't help smiling.

Tanya and I are dressed up, shiny shoes and our hair just so. People are spilling out into the kitchen and the backyard.

Mummy's an amazing dancer. Hips sway, shoulders jerk, and rock-steady footwork. Rhythm and soul. I'm watching her possessed by the sounds, lifting her arms past her shoulders reaching to the popcorn ceiling. Her smile. "Shine like a Cheshire cat," they said about her smile.

The lights are getting dim, and there's a slow-motion smile in the room, a friendly slurring. Tanya and I get sent to bed and it's hard to sleep, the bass rattling the walls and the glassware in the cabinet. We sneak out of our beds and peek around the corner to watch everyone slow dancing, arms up in the air, eyes closed, bellies full, laughing. Next week it will happen just so.

A friend, too tipsy to drive home, has slept in the spare room. The furniture's still moved, and Tanya and I take advantage of the space to dance all morning.

At fifteen, I started partying in Miami with Tanya and our friends. My crew of close friends (Amanda, Maria, Mikey, Dorlis, Vicky, Alexis, Kim, Andre, Steven) were all a little outside the box, outcasts in a way, some of them first-generation immigrant kids. A kind of forgetting was common in the houses of my friends—forget your past, become American. Maybe it's a common immigrant story.

We went to raves, and I loved the feeling of the music and the vibration, the rebellious edge to it, the illegal venues and the psychedelic drugs. Miami was grittier and edgier, and I craved it.

We knew a lot of kids who were either selling drugs, using, or abusing. My sister was pretty protective of me, so I didn't have the option to experiment until she left for college. I didn't get addicted to drugs, but I enjoyed them. I was addicted to dancing and music.

Tanya and I were obsessed with a record store called Uncle Sam's. Wearing her tennis skirt, fishnet stockings, and black eyeliner, or baggy jeans with chain belt, Tanya's tugging at my shirt, rolling up my pants, and latching my collar just right. Nineties raver fashion.

"You never know who you'll meet at Uncle Sam's," she says.

There were rows and rows of blue wooden album displays, record player stations with headphones attached, used cassette walls, and selections of paraphernalia, from concert T-shirts, bongs, and pipes to Dr. Martens boots. Uncle Sam's had it all, and it was our beacon, our source for new music.

We begged Mummy to take us to Uncle Sam's, and we begged her to wait in the car. Both of us not knowing how young we were, so eager to grow. Experiment. Needing her hand and not wanting it.

When I think of Uncle Sam's, I see myself meeting Marilyn Manson, him signing Tanya's lunch box. Listening to DJ Josh Wink live, buying tickets to the first ever Lollapalooza.

Growing up quickly.

Outside of their parties, my parents were hard-working and strict. I credit them for my work ethic, but there were times as a teenager when life in Plantation felt a little closed in. When I was at school or anywhere away from home, I figured out how to just be myself, and I found I could fit in almost everywhere. That has served me well throughout my life. The more I went to Miami, dancing, smoking pot, the more strict my parents became, always asking questions about where I was going and who I was with. It started to make the suburban side of Plantation feel like more of a trap.

Around that time I picked up a camera, and things started to change.

My dad was into photography, and we had a collection of cameras in the house. He once had a job at a photo studio in Jamaica when he was a teenager, and he fell in love with taking pictures. I picked up a camera and fell in love, too. Shooting portraits, trying to capture unseen sides of people. My dad explained composition and what made a good picture, and I learned that capturing real emotions was the hard but crucial part. A picture I was proud of at the time was a close-up of a little Black boy on a swing in a park, runny nose and wide eyes. I'd asked his mum if I could take his picture, she nodded, and I caught some cross between despair and contentment in the boy—him seeing new possibility in the moment having just cried his eyes out. A glimpse of innocence and Black joy.

It was devastating for me when Tanya left for college.

When I was younger, there was tension in the house over Daddy's late nights, him spending every Saturday night at the Domino Club, the music, women, dancing. Both of my parents' pasts were weighted with having other children and other relationships, and try as they did to live these new days, the past was alive whether they liked it or not.

My dad had three kids with his first wife, Faye. Joy, Oneil, and Wayne. Mummy, too, had a son, another Wayne, before she met my dad.

"Who's going to help me with Mummy and Daddy? They don't understand me."

Tanya was my protector, my voice of reason.

"You'll be fine," she said. "Don't get angry with them."

In hindsight, I totally respect my parents' decision to build a home in Plantation. They wanted the security of a quiet neighbourhood, a "safe" place to enrich their daughters' childhood and forget their past struggles in their journeys as immigrants. But as a slightly rebellious teenager, I felt like they were living with blinders on, not seeing the adventures and possibilities. Tanya and I saw some of it walking and dancing in the streets of Miami, but we both craved more. I couldn't wait to get out, away from the chain restaurants, the strip malls, the too-quiet neighbourhood that was repetitive, stagnant.

Just before graduation, I applied to art school: the School of Visual Arts New York City.

I wanted to be an artist. I yearned for self-expression, and my camera was my tool. I wasn't so interested in academics or pure study, but I wasn't just going to get a job straight out of high school. It was a risk applying to only one school, but for whatever reason I had a hunch. My mind was set.

"Mummy, I want to go to art school in New York."

Me on one of the stools. Mummy chopping onions.

She kisses her teeth.

"What's wrong with school here in Florida? Where you going to live?"

Turns out she couldn't have been more supportive.

"Let me see what I can do."

I think she was forced to do many things in her life that she didn't want to do: move to England, get married, leave her son, move to Florida, work as a cleaner for extra money, other jobs she didn't love. She didn't want me to settle for less or to follow a path that felt inauthentic. Artistic expression was important to her. She loved ceramics and interior design—it was all there in how she built our house.

I felt a spark bounce off her chest—she would do whatever was possible to make my dream a reality.

My father wasn't so sure. What kind of a job could I get with an arts degree? He didn't want his youngest daughter living in New York City. It's dangerous, it's raw, it's running away. "She can stay here and go to community college and figure out her next steps," he said. I'm sure they had more heated discussions about my jobless future.

My mum ended up paying my first semester's tuition with her own credit card. Secretly. I found out after she died.

She believed in me, and that helped me believe in myself.

I'm trying to picture my mum in London. She's at a club for teen-agers, called the Flamingo, that's only open on Sunday nights. I imagine the walls covered in posters from dance parties and promo pictures of legendary artists. The smell of stale beer, tattered carpets and unbuffed dark wood floors, velvet rope barriers pulled from the closet where they usually lie next to the mop and broom. The DJ plays the slower tunes to get the crowd settled in. It's about to be on. Tempo rising, and the bass is bumping.

Her back to the wall, her smile lights up the room, and she's dancing. A tall young man named Roy swaggers in wearing a fedora. A hustler, my mum's friend Ivy calls him. A show-off. A good dancer, who probably says all the right things. It's the six-ties, and they're the children of what's become known as the Windrush generation.

In 1948, 802 Caribbean immigrants land at Tilbury Dock in Essex County, England, on a ship called *Empire Windrush*, and the wave of Caribbean people who settle in the city are known by the name of the ship. My mum's dad is among the many who work on the railroad, hoping to create a better life for his family.

Even though they have full rights, they face all kinds of prejudice and abuse. Black men are attacked in the streets, many are denied housing, and if you can't get one of those jobs with British Rail, there aren't many doors open for you.

Find your bars, your cafés, your community. Those two teenagers dancing at the Flamingo are being themselves, looking for escape and identity just like I will in Plantation. "I want to be American," he says. Holding her close.

He has a complicated mind, a street man looking for an angle. I don't know if he is my mum's first love, and most of what I know of him I will learn from her dearest friend, Ivy, who doesn't like him from the get-go.

It doesn't matter what anyone says; Mummy is smitten. He calls her "Star," and she shines like a supernova. Ivy and my grandmother tell my mum to stay away from him, and Ivy and Mummy have a falling-out because of it. "Bad man," my grandmother says.

As soon as she gets pregnant, everything changes. It's unacceptable for a girl to be pregnant and not married, so they get hitched. And from there, things get worse.

Did she want to marry him? Separating love and lust at such a young age is difficult. Maybe she just liked the attention he gave her. I go back to that wedding photo. Her eyes. They fought a lot, and he abused my mum and was with other women who had kids with him.

My Aunt Hilgay tells a story about my brother Wayne as a baby. Hilgay was ten and my mother twenty. She was in the house with my mum and her husband and the baby. Mummy and Roy are upstairs with Wayne, and they're fighting. It gets louder, the yelling and screaming. Loud thuds and smashed glass. Hilgay is watching TV, unsure of what to do, when my mum comes tearing down the stairs, through the TV room, and throws Wayne toward her. My aunt catches him in mid-air. Mummy keeps running straight out the door, in fear for her life. Within a few months, she's on her way to Canada to be with her eldest sister, Lurline. Wayne stays in England with our grandmother and the rest of my mum's family.

So from that night at the Flamingo comes a boy who lives in England for his first eight years without his mum. Then he comes to Canada, leaving school, friends, and family, and gets picked up in a big orange convertible by my dad, his new father, and he tries to adapt to this culture that my parents themselves are still new to.

That image of Wayne flying through the air has stayed with me. There's something symbolic about it. Being between two worlds. We share the same blood and he's someone I want to know, thrown by circumstance into a tougher life than Tanya and I knew. In a new country, missing London, trying to find his place in Toronto, he slowly grew more comfortable with his Canadian family. His cousin, Terry, became his best friend. It was Wayne who named both me and

Tanya. He says he was excited to have siblings and remembers those years in Canada as good, once he got over missing England. He was surrounded by a new family in Toronto, many of them from the UK.

Like my mum and Tanya, Wayne is reserved and takes control of his emotions. As a kid, he didn't want to cause any problems. He accepted life and circumstances as they came to him. He wanted to get along with everyone.

And then he was made to move again. This time to Florida.

I talk to him on the phone.

"I used to bump into a lot of guys," he says. "We'd sit there, somebody would introduce something new, you'd try it out . . . coke . . . I used to keep my head about me . . . I don't think I ever tried any real hard drugs. I guess it was weed at the start, and when that made me too paranoid, it was the coke. I used to hang out in Royal Palm . . . Zack was my best friend. We went to a party one night and there was an altercation with the guys we were with. Me and Zack went running up, and the guys started shooting. And inevitably the bullet caught Zack in the neck, who was right beside me, and he ended up dying . . . And I don't know, I just did weird things from there. At that time I'd not seen a person get shot, I'd not seen a person just lying there, but when . . . He had a hoodie on, and once they pulled it back to find where he'd been hit, they found it in his neck. So . . . I was probably about seventeen, Zack was eighteen. Zack Moton. I guess I just went numb. I went to the funeral, I remember looking at him, and that's the first time I looked at someone I would have known in a casket."

"And where did it go for you after that? You were in high school, you weren't sure of what to do . . . ?" I ask.

"I think I just more or less turned numb to it. Most of the guys I was with in high school, a lot were getting shot, a lot were going to prison, a lot were turning into crackheads. So there were a couple that I knew from Boyd Anderson high school, and I saw them later on and they'd sell you anything."

Wayne started spending more time on the street with his friends than at home with us. Maybe he was looking for a different kind of support, a freedom that was impossible to find living with Mummy and Daddy. At twenty-two years old, Wayne ended up going to prison for possession of crack cocaine.

This was 1986, when Ronald Reagan was doubling down on the war on drugs (and cutting social services in predominantly Black neighbourhoods across the country). Government and the media were sensationalizing a made-up "crack epidemic." Prison sentences for holding one gram of crack cocaine were suddenly a hundred times as long as sentences for holding one gram of powder cocaine. Crack is cheaper to produce, so it's cheaper to buy, and it became more accessible in poor, Black, urban communities. Black people were being disproportionately targeted (many of them boys and men) by the police who were trying to stop the "epidemic."

"The court brought me in," Wayne said. "I didn't care anymore, I guess I just thought what's going to happen is going to happen. For that year, I was in Hendry Correctional Institution, and after that the Immigration Center."

Wayne told his girlfriend to keep it all a secret, and she did. We didn't know where he was; he was just absent from our lives. There's a hole in my gut when I think of that. I don't know how much my parents knew, but they didn't talk about it in front of Tanya and me.

The next time I saw him, Mummy was telling me to put on my best clothes and to get in the car. I was ten years old. It was still dark when we started our drive, and everything felt dreamlike. Four a.m., and my blouse and skirt were uncomfortable. I wanted my pajamas. Mummy was remote and tense. I had no idea what was going on. The highway was quiet, and the gentle vibrations of the car put me back to sleep. And then we were there.

We parked our car in a designated parking lot and boarded a bus that took us to the Immigration Center. From the window of the shuttle, I saw the sun start to rise, its warm yellow rays lighting the already blue sky. It was beautiful. We got off the bus and joined a line of people being shuffled through security gates, where our

bodies were checked and our bags of gifts for the detainees were also rummaged through and examined. We were escorted into an open area where we sat and waited for my brother.

I watched each man coming through a door in the corner of the room, scanned his face to see if I recognized him. Finally it was Wayne, dressed like all the other men in an orange jumpsuit. I felt scared. We stood up to greet him. He seemed unbothered, taciturn. I can't remember what I said to him, but I remember saying "I love you" when we left. And that was it. It was a short visit, and soon after, Wayne was sent back to England.

Was it a broken home for him, or did he have a broken, lost heart longing for something he didn't or couldn't ask for? He wasn't a lost cause, just a misunderstood child who wanted to be loved and accepted.

In Plantation, Wayne fought a lot with Mummy and Daddy. There was always something, and they were tough on him. When he started spending more time on the street, their trust was broken. He was old enough to make his own decisions and choices, whether the path he was on was sustainable or not.

When we left the facility, Mummy walked heavy with guilt. She was leaving her son once again, and she was not able to protect him from the distractions that absorbed him.

Looking back, I recognize that I had a less disrupted childhood than Wayne. I still feel guilty about that.

That Florida sun rose up through my high school days, and I left it behind for New York.

I cut out my perm and dyed my hair blonde for my high school graduation. Tight curls, professionally dyed. I knew that changing my look completely would seem radical to my parents, so I didn't tell them. As a teenager on the verge of finding her own path, I wasn't going to ask for permission.

Hair for Black women is everything. It's a part of our identity, our freedom, and our sexuality. And our power. I felt that so clearly that day. Changing my hair was a huge step toward finding my independence.

I dressed at a friend's house and went straight to the rented amphitheatre for the ceremony. It wasn't until I walked across the stage that I saw my parents' shocked reactions. I think they realized that they no longer had control over me. My dad's silent disapproval was mixed with his pride for the occasion. My mum was indifferent. "Your hair," she said. She smirked at me. I think she knew how important this change was for me to stand out from the crowd and establish my style, my flow.

Two months before, I had been accepted into the School of Visual Arts. I was moving to Manhattan! And I was stoked. No more Plantation. No more parents asking constant questions. I wanted some freedom, and New York seemed the perfect place to find that. Big city, millions of people, countless streets to explore. Every neighbourhood felt mythical: Harlem, SoHo, Hell's Kitchen. I'd heard stories about all of them in film and books.

Fall semester was already full, so I was starting in the winter of 1996. I couldn't wait those six months to find that freedom, though, so I moved in with Tanya in Tallahassee. Working as a telemarketer for the local paper, I took my first deep breaths as an adult.

I landed at LaGuardia in a snowstorm. Mummy was concerned for my safety in NYC, so I'd compromised and agreed to live in an all-female dorm, right across the street from Gramercy Park on 21st Street. We were between the bustling avenues of Park and Lexington, and we had the keys to a private garden that was shared with a dozen other brownstones, a quiet haven amid the madness of Manhattan.

One of my roommates was a Chinese American girl, Mai, who was a painter and in her third year. She introduced me to seaweed, a food I'd never tried before. Nori and rice became a favourite dish, and it opened my hunger for many other flavours that I found in NYC. The city is such an incredible amalgam of cultures, and I started to seek out other cuisines I was unfamiliar with. Inexpensive Mom-and-Pop holes in the wall were my favourite. Late-night shawarma, saag paneer, falafel, North African food, Mexican, pupusas in Queens, black-and-white cookies on Lexington Avenue.

New York taught me about how food could be deeply tied to cultural expression. Food was a way to get to know the city—and the people in it—and I loved that. It excited me.

I kept my short blonde afro. I was nineteen, and it was the first time I felt free to really live my life as I wanted to. I remember climbing the stairs to the dorm roof early one morning to find the whole city blanketed in snow. There were lots of blizzards that year, and I always felt chilled, but that morning the sun was out, and it was so quiet up there. The frozen city was radiant.

I was out with my camera all the time in the Lower East Side and Alphabet City, taking photos of shapes, shadows, and architecture. Photography became less about portraits and faces for me, and more about exploring different spaces. Maybe it had to do with my bubbling questions about how people took up space, and what spaces people were allowed to inhabit. I went to countless galleries and museums and started seeing Black and female photographers who shot the civil rights movement and politically charged historical moments. Louis Draper, Gordon Parks, and Fannie Lou Hamer moved me with the way they captured people in space.

Most of my classes were great, but I was learning way more outside the classroom.

Near the end of the semester, Mummy called to say that she couldn't afford to pay for the next semester. I would need to get a job and figure out a plan. Or maybe I could come home and she could save up and then I could go back.

This is where the hustle part of my life started as I tried to make enough money to stay in the city and to grow as an artist. School tuition felt like an extravagance, and I figured I didn't really need classes because the whole city was my classroom.

I got a job as an assistant for a photographer named Rebecca McKnight. While I was working for Rebecca, though, my mother's sister, Lurline, passed away from pancreatic cancer and I started questioning everything.

I made the one-hour flight to Toronto to attend the funeral. I reconnected with my extended family. And I saw my mother completely broken. She was so close to Lurline, her big sister who saved her when she was sent from London to Canada.

When I returned to NYC, I was deeply sad. I was terrified of losing my own sister, and I missed my family. NYC is electric, but it's expensive. Finding money to pay the rent took more energy than I wanted. Having less time to make art started to take a toll on me. *Why am I here?* The student life I had in NYC had changed, and I was changing. My new reality coincided with Tanya moving to Atlanta. "Come live with me, come to Atlanta," she said.

I'd heard the term "Black mecca" when people referred to Atlanta, and it always interested me as a city. Atlanta had been associated with Black success in politics, business, and culture, and I wanted to experience what that felt like. New York had opened me up to culture through photography, food, music, painting, and film, but at some level, the experience felt incomplete or interfered with, compromised. There was a Black American experience I hadn't yet known.

I knew I wasn't done with New York forever.

That time of life when the body and soul are growing in a richer way, and these desires, this confidence, these questions build . . . You feel yourself, your limits growing, and you want deeper friends, want to find yourself in a community. You become a woman.

In the spring of 1997, friends of mine organized a trip to join the Million Woman March in Philadelphia. I stood in the crowd taking photos, and the women all around me literally lifted me up. They put me on top of a loudspeaker to get better shots as I listened to Maxine Waters's message of hope and strength.

*I am here today to speak for my mother, her mother, and her mother's mother. The mothers that have long passed and the mothers born into slavery. I speak for Black women and girls! For women that claim colour and those confused about colour.*

I felt goosebumps slowly rise with each word.

From the top of the speaker, I saw a sea of Black women, and it was at that point that I first felt a need to become an advocate. I could have a voice, and I felt the strength of the bonds you can make when you work together. The power I had at that point in my life was using my camera to share my vision. I thought about my own mother, and her mother, and I left that day with a commitment to honour them by continuing to become a strong Black woman. I wanted to surround myself with Black culture: music, literature, film, and visual arts.

Along the way and through the march there was such great energy. Motivating stories from so many women introduced me to Black feminism at a deeper level than I'd known, and they opened my mind to sensuality. It connected me to myself as a Black woman, and the power of my worth.

The musician Erykah Badu was living in Atlanta at the time. She was a proud woman using her voice and artistry to tell her story. She wrapped her hair in cloth, celebrating African culture and heritage, and she led the neo-soul movement. She helped me see myself not just as Canadian and Jamaican, but African. She embodied for so many of us this return to Africa: a beautiful liberated Black woman making all Black women beautiful, calling us to action. Her album *Baduizm* was the soundtrack to my Atlanta life. She personified the type of Black experience I was looking for.

At the time I also learned more about Rastafarianism, and I became a vegan for a while. I started thinking more about food as medicine. The Rasta's Ital cuisine dictates that whatever food you put in your body should serve to enliven and enlighten.

And so here I am, in a loft in downtown Atlanta. Old industrial build-ing converted into live/work spaces. High ceilings, worn leather couches, the back wall a series of steel-framed windows. The place is full of turntables, mics, video game consoles, and other gear. A recording booth off to the side. The loft is owned by A-live, Message, and I-Rap, three dope musicians.

I'm heavily into hip-hop and drum and bass. Mos Def, Common, Nas, the Roots, and Kemistry and Storm. I've been looking for my crew, people into the same music. My DJ friend Riddim, back in NYC, is hugely connected and he sets me up in Atlanta. He con-nects me to A-live, who opens up the world to me.

I'm hanging out at the loft a lot. More than I'm at home. It's a hub, a hive, a place where I can almost relax if I can ignore the cre-ative energy and the buzz I feel in this yearning body. Any musician coming to perform hip-hop in Atlanta comes here, in through that door; doors in my mind opening to new ways of seeing and being. True brotherhood here, parties and shared beats.

I'm taking photos of everyone. While we circle, talk, and feel the fires through late-night cyphers and midnight recording sessions. It's my local. I've been going to underground hip-hop shows with my camera around my neck and I've become a regular.

Dreams of going to Clark Atlanta University. My mum has called and told me that they can't afford to help me out. I'm weirdly relieved. This is my school. Find my own way. Make mistakes and learn deeper from those than from classes.

I'm dating Cubes, a total character, comic-book loyalist, hip-hop fanatic, performer. Late nights and laughing my ass off. And all those surprises walking through that door.

He's a mastermind on the lyrics. Not Cubes, but Patrick. He gets those goosebumps up again, the skin on my arms pulling me up to dance. Patrick's known as I-Rap, and he's one of the room-mates at the loft.

My fun times with Cubes come to an end and here I am falling for Patrick, his words. He's an incredibly talented musician and dancer, and he talks and dances out his dreams, and I'm there with him, right there, like a believer. He's got me. And I've got him. He's older, much older, and I like that. He asks me questions, listens, respects my opinions. When I talk about music, art, food, politics, he's with my words like I'm with his.

Days and nights I'm working on film ideas. I'm hanging out with Patrick, going to shows with my camera. I'm working at Tomorrow Pictures with my mentor, filmmaker Frederick Taylor, first as a personal assistant, then an office assistant, and I start submitting Fred's work to film festivals. Seeing how films are made, how ideas change through that long journey from camera to screen—the whole process totally fascinates me.

And Patrick inspires me, every one of those days and nights. So creative. Teaching me what it means to live an artistic life.

He's the one.

I'm in the loft, I'm back at the house I'm sharing with Tanya, and all the time I'm catching myself thinking about these things: wife; mother; artist. Yes!

There's respect. Right from the beginning. I support him, he sup-ports me. He's the only man I've introduced to my mum. Blur and hum and the beat of days, each more important than any day before, and here we are, two years up the mountain, and I'm pregnant.

Boom.

It's a shock. It brings me down to the street again, for a second, but it doesn't take long for us to get excited. You're suspended in those days that never end when you're in love like that, a timeless place, and then here it is: a future, time, a path you have to notice. Patrick already has a daughter and he never sees her. There's a reality here. But, still, the reality looks sweet.

All of it so short.

So quick.

I'm looking at that girl dreaming.

Woman, yes, becoming, but still a girl if I can be honest. Just cut loose from the apron strings, trying to figure it out, stretching and growing, no doubt, but a girl. I'm dreaming of going to LA and making it in the film world, wanting to keep that hum going, keep opening those doors. I'm just getting started. How can I have a baby?

"Get Patrick to call me."

I say that a lot. Patrick is on tour, and I keep asking A-live: "Can you get Patrick to call me?" I'm having this vision: two years down the road, three years, ten; he's still on tour, he's always on tour, and I'm alone with our child.

For the first few days of his tour we talk on the phone all the time. Then less. Once a week. He stops answering emails, texts. I keep telling A-live, "Get Patrick to call me." I know nothing about his relationship with the mother of his daughter. It's like she doesn't exist. How are we going to be any different? It's all coming at me and what I feel in the middle of it is my hands reaching out for things I can't quite reach, watching doors close instead of open, and trying, trying to breathe. Not a woman yet, and my freedom and life are over.

I thought about calling my mum, but the shame was too heavy. It was the first big secret I kept from her. I didn't tell my sister. I didn't tell anyone. It would be on me to accept this decision; it was my choice and I didn't know what else to do. I was scared. And I had to act quickly.

I sat in the waiting room, faded pink paint on the walls. It was a family care facility, so there were a couple of toys in the corners.

Straight-backed chairs from the eighties. My name was called, and when I was in the next room, the doctor appeared, neither cold nor warm. She asked if I wanted a mild anesthesia, but I refused as I wanted to remember the whole process. This would be my pain. The doctor asked if I wanted the nurse to stay, and I said yes. I didn't know exactly what the procedure involved. My feet were in stirrups. Everything went silent. The doctor's voice was distant as I stared up at a brown water stain in the drop ceiling. When the intense pressure started, I reached for the nurse's hand. Instead of offering it she gave me a tension ball.

Life coming out of me. Giving up on Patrick. Giving up on us. I hated myself. It was less than ten minutes. I had my own life back, and I was numb.

"There will be some bleeding, but you can take Advil or Tylenol for the pain."

The only person I had confided in was a co-worker who picked me up. I sat in the car paralyzed. I cried all night.

"Baby, I'm back."

The tour was over. It was 10 o'clock at night. There were too many people at his place, so I took him down to my car.

"You fucking bitch," he said.

"Fuck you," I said.

It would break us, this fight. Sadness, so much pain and regret. A-live yelled out the window, "You need to stop."

Weeks passed and we tried with apologies but we both realized that it was over. The love and trust were a distant memory. A few months later I packed my stuff and drove back to Florida.

My mother and father kept secrets. And maybe to them they weren't so much secrets as things they needed to hide to get by. To move on.

When I ask my dad to remember things, I'm not sure whether he really doesn't want to or whether forgetting them has just become part of his identity. How he survived.

I've never stopped running from one thing to another. But I'm trying to remember.

For the entire second year I was in Atlanta, my mum complained about back pain.

"My back is bothering me, but I'll be fine. How are you and Patrick doing? Tell Tanya to call me, please."

Her doctor first diagnosed it as an ulcer. They needed more tests. But in her voice it felt like it was more. She knew it was more. She called me shortly after my fight with Patrick.

"I have cancer."

She had been diagnosed with pancreatic cancer. This would be a fight; we prepared for battle.

*Ginger root.*
*Cerasee leaves.*
*Peppermint.*
*Bay leaf.*
*Nutmeg.*
*Cloves.*
*A little honey.*

Start with ginger in the bottom of the pot. Slowly add aromatics—cerasee leaves, peppermint and bay leaf, then dried nutmeg shavings, seeds and stems of the cloves. Fill the pot with water. Add honey. Stir and lower the flame.

Bush tea will heal all that ails.

Sip night and day.

# TWO

# LEAVING

When coconut fall from tree he can't fasten back

I was home again. A mess of shame, relief, and fear. Should I tell her? I wanted to. I wanted her to hug me and to tell me everything was okay. That my decision to end the pregnancy wasn't selfish or wrong. I wanted that weight off my shoulders. I wanted her to understand.

I stood underneath the kitchen's skylight in a rectangle of warmth. She was in the living room on the couch, drinking Earl Grey tea. The words never came. I guess I feared her judgment. And when I realized how sick she was, she became my priority. I tried not to think about Patrick and the abortion and hoped the memories would fade. I was back in my old bedroom—now a guest room—my leftover belongings pushed to the back of the closet. I found remnants of high school in the gold-trimmed dresser: a thrift shop T-shirt, one-piece bathing suits, a vintage summer dress riddled with distressed holes. The wallpaper border of pink, yellow, and purple flowers that I always hated was one of the only things that remained. And the ackee tree out the window.

I unpacked my suitcase and stayed for more than a year.

Tanya's room was empty, and I missed sitting on her bed with her, talking about anything. She was living in New York, travelling back and forth to see Mummy. The house felt quiet, like it was holding its breath. My mum still cleaned—she couldn't help it—and the rooms were tidy, but there was a thin layer of dust on everything.

Soon the days were full of doctors' appointments and hospital visits. Atlanta felt like a distant memory.

Her GP initially thought she had a broken rib, then an ulcer, but when the pain didn't get any better, he ordered an MRI and they discovered pancreatic cancer. It was the same cancer her sister, Lurline, had died from, and we were stunned that the doctor hadn't suspected it was cancer earlier. I was angry about how it was handled. We all were. We considered suing the doctor for malpractice, but ultimately we redirected all that rage into helping her fight the cancer. Still, I couldn't help but think that treatment done a year earlier might have prolonged, or even saved, her life. Anything to believe.

After the diagnosis, she had surgery to remove a tumour in her pancreas, and then began chemotherapy and radiation. Mummy and I got up early each morning, she put on her dress shorts, T-shirt, and a cardigan, and I drove her to Hollywood, Florida. With jewellery on, and lipstick, too, Monday to Friday, our mornings were spent in the air-conditioned oncology clinic where they pumped medicine into her veins and we all hoped for the best. We didn't speak a lot back then. She couldn't speak. The drugs were so powerful.

My mum was a beautiful woman. Everyone said so. She always spent time on her appearance—her clothes were always proper and her makeup done. *Cleanliness is next to godliness*. Each week she'd get her hair done at Glenda's Hair Salon, the chair in the back of Glenda's house. She'd often bring me and Tanya along, and we'd play with Glenda's kids while Glenda worked her magic. Mum's hair was central to her notion of femininity. The possibility of losing her hair was devastating, and she had it cut into a shorter style so the hair loss would be less dramatic.

Before the diagnosis, my mum had gained a lot of weight as she couldn't move around comfortably because of the back pain. During treatment she lost it all. She became pale and thin, and her eyes looked hollow.

Exhausted, she often slept with her head against the window on the drive home, highway, strip malls, and ocean speeding by.

We got home and I tried to feed her. Her appetite was off, but I tried rice and chicken, maybe some kind of sandwich. She couldn't eat.

Standing in that kitchen I knew so well, I realized I didn't have a clue how to feed her. I always loved to cook, but this time was different. I was trying to cook from a place of memory, but I couldn't remember anything.

"Mummy, are you hungry?"

A grunt and a moan signalled that she wasn't in any state to eat. I remember offering her steamed broccoli, parboiled rice, baked chicken legs. If Daddy was home, he blessed us with curry chicken, rice and peas, or cow-foot soup. Those dishes sat in front of her untouched as the fat congealed and formed a skin on top along with the allspice and thyme stems. Mummy attempted to eat the food she loved, but she couldn't keep it down. She'd spent her whole life feeding us and I didn't know how to make her favourite foods, or meals that would fortify her for cancer treatment. I watched my parents cook, yes, but I didn't know the techniques or their recipes. And I wasn't even sure what her body needed. I wanted to give her comfort, but I also wanted to give her the right kind of nourishment. I failed at both.

The only thing she always said yes to was tea. She never added sweetener to her tea. The hot caffeinated water was the only thing that seemed to bring her comfort.

My mum became a tea lover in England. She loved the ritual of it, the way making a pot of tea could organize time. The warmth of it calmed her. And I loved making it for her. When I was a kid, after she got home from work, I put the stovetop kettle on to boil and grabbed her favourite teacup from the cupboard. She loved Red Rose and Lipton black teas. I took a bag from the glass container on the counter and placed it in the cup. I warmed the cup with hot tap water first, then poured milk in the bottom to be tempered by the boiling water. The colour had to be perfect—she liked it to be a light caramel shade—not too strong, but still strong enough for a hint of bitterness. She sat on the couch with her feet up, closing her eyes when I brought her the cup. She would breathe in the steam, then take a tiny sip.

She didn't want to spend her days in bed. She left the blinds open. She slept on the couch sometimes, but for her it was about keeping her composure and finding some kind of control. Sitting upright on the couch as if she was settled, feet planted solidly on the carpet as she watched *Judge Judy*. Her wrinkled forehead was the only indication of pain. People still came to visit, and she smiled like the gracious hostess she always was.

My dad had a book bindery business at the time and worked long hours, so he wasn't always around in the kitchen to help. He seemed to avoid our home and my mum because he couldn't deal with her pain or her anger. When she wasn't quiet, she was full of fury. All the resentment she felt toward my father that had built up over the years came out. Leaving her family in Canada. Her guilt and sadness about Wayne. She hated the fact that my father went out all the time, leaving her to look after Tanya and me. She wanted to spend time with him, to go dancing and for dinner. That rarely happened. I think she blamed him for her cancer. She blamed him for a lot of her pain.

Her friend Ivy remembers calling my mum from Toronto on my parents' anniversary. My mum was crying because he was out playing dominos with friends. "She kept most things inside her," Ivy says. "She was a strong person but she kept a lot inside."

I'd see my dad early in the morning before work, and he was always a bit distant. He continued to provide for our family. He just wasn't prepared for Mummy's illness. I was left to care for Mummy on my own, and it was intense. I'm so grateful I had that time with her, but it was challenging.

There was a lot of love between my parents. I saw it throughout my life. But I also saw them fight, and sometimes they didn't communicate at all. Mummy's illness could have brought them closer, but there was just too much fear and sadness and repressed anger for that to happen. It breaks my heart when I think about it. If only I could have done something to help.

The house clean.

The air still. Stale.

On the couch was the indentation of her body. By the couch was a bucket in case she was sick. The TV was almost always on, white and blue light flickering on the medicine bottles.

Everyone felt trapped. Alone.

I stood there with the fridge door open surveying its contents. Maybe if I could make her favourite meals from childhood, she'd be able to eat. Steamed mackerel with peppers and yams. Beef liver and onions. Escovitch fish and bammy. But I didn't know how to make any of them. I couldn't even remember the details of her ackee and saltfish.

I tried to summon my grandmothers, my ancestors. I told my hands to create something comforting, sentimental. It didn't work. How can I make my mum feel better? I had an understanding that food could be medicine. I saw it all my life. Food could be the thing that ended fights between my parents, it could be the thing that helped a sour belly, that made an eye infection better. I just didn't know what kind of medicine my mum needed.

Taking care of anyone is a difficult job, and I eventually needed to escape the pressure. I signed up for some photography and women's studies classes at Florida International University. I wanted to get back to the things that I was interested in. There was a relief in thinking about things other than my mum, but there was a different kind of relief stepping back into the house after class and seeing her smile.

I took a photo of her standing outside the oncologist's office the day she finished her treatment, and we found out she was cancer-free. She was wearing her blue dress shorts and a crisp, white cotton shirt. Her hair was cut close to her head, and although her eyes were tired, she was happy. The chemo had done its job.

There were a few months of calm and positivity, and then we were given the worst news imaginable. Cancer had spread to her liver and her spine, and it was making its way to her brain. She grew even thinner. Her body was failing.

Near the end of her life, hospice brought a hospital bed to the house and we set it up next to the king-sized bed in her bedroom. My dad slept on the other side of the house in the guest room because he was still working and didn't want to disturb her sleep. It was all too painful for him.

The TV is on, that ghostly blue dancing across her face. It's late at night, and I'm sitting up in bed watching her watch some rerun of an eighties sitcom. *The Jeffersons* or 227. We do this every night. Her eyes close, and then they open, and I hope for a restful sleep that never comes. My heart hurts.

The doctor has prescribed oxycontin in liquid form because her pain has reached a new intensity. He gave me the bottle with a warning to be careful as the drug was ten times as powerful as the pills she'd been taking. The drug eases the pain for a while, and then she starts moaning as her discomfort increases.

I put some of the medicine into her mouth and we both sleep for a time, and then her moans wake me up. Another dose. She sleeps and I guess I do too. Her moans turn to cries, and I'm so tired. I start crying too. "Please stop. Please stop crying, Mummy."

She's suddenly silent.

I jump out of bed and turn on the light. My heart's racing. I shake her shoulders and then run down the hallway to my dad. I'm terrified that I've given her an overdose.

My dad calls 911, and the ambulance arrives soon after. The paramedics decide to take her to hospital and I follow in Mummy's car. Daddy goes to the office to sort something out before joining me there.

The sun's coming up, those first few rays turning the black sky blue.

She's in the hospice ward, fluorescent-lit hallway leading to a room with faded walls. Hooked up to an IV, a ventilator, and a heart monitor, her body seems so small. Daddy's there, and then he's not. The doctor says there's nothing more they can do. I call Tanya to tell her to come home.

Sitting at the foot of the bed, I watch my half-conscious mum try to pull out the IV and the mask on her face. She clutches at her hospital gown, trying to pull it off, gasping for air. Her arm reaches up and her gaze is fixed on something behind me. She takes a few more breaths, and then her last. I'm there, alone in her room when my mother dies.

*I stand here now as your daughter,*
*a sister, and a mother.*

*I remember Sunday dinners.*

After my mum's death, I stayed in Plantation with my dad for a little while, but there was a lot of tension between us and he eventually kicked me out.

He started dating a woman named Junie who was a relative of one of his best friends from Canada, and I wasn't ready for that. It felt like he was trying to replace my mother. I didn't blame her. I blamed him. He's a man with needs and he was hurting, disconnected from his emotions. My father is a proud man, a provider, and a scared young boy still lives within him.

Betrayal might be too harsh a word, but it felt like that to me. He was betraying the memory of my mum. Couldn't he see that he was doing the exact thing he had hated his own mother for doing when his father died? Did my dad feel that same sense of betrayal that I felt with him? Could he remember it?

I don't think he was ready for the emptiness of the house, and his heart. Sonny and Nicey. He'd bring up moments from early in their relationship, like he was trying to burn them into his memory.

I feel like we failed each other. We didn't allow one another to mourn her, to celebrate her spirit, and I ended up crossing a line that many Caribbean kids will understand: "Fuck you." It was pure emotion, deep anger. As the "you" left my lips and landed on his face, I knew I could never take it back. He had just told me that Junie was moving into our house after my mother had been gone for less than six months.

I moved to Miami. I tried to reset. I was still stunned by her death. At the funeral I didn't cry. Relatives said *you'll cry one day*. I'd been crying every day for a year. Every night.

Those days in Miami were a blur, but work gave me some kind of focus. These jobs led to an opportunity at the MTV network in New York City. It was a good thing for me mentally as I associated NYC with opportunity and independence, and those were two things I needed more than ever at that point in my life. I needed a new view out my window and new thoughts to fill my brain. I flew north again.

I started working in MTV's off-air design department, where we made those wacky commercials that featured the MTV logo. I started as a production coordinator/manager and within six months, my boss told me that she was resigning and she was recommending me as the new line producer for the department. A big jump. And it all happened so fast. How could she think I was ready to run the department's million-dollar budget?

I called Tanya one Monday morning on my way into the office, crying. What the hell did I know about this job? I felt totally unprepared for the responsibilities required, and I didn't know what to do. What she told me continues to serve me well today. "Don't let this opportunity pass without giving it all you can. If you don't know every aspect of your role, go in early and stay late. Learn."

And that's what I did. I started my days before sunrise and left my five-by-five cubicle after sunset. I sat in on budget meetings and read reports. I talked to people in other departments, and with my production manager, Samantha, next to me, we created an incredible small team. MTV taught me that you're never going to be fully prepared for anything, but don't let that stop you. I learned to project confidence, even if I didn't always feel it. And I learned that I can do anything if I put my mind to it. I can't say that it was my dream job, and working for a corporate behemoth like Viacom didn't jibe with my sensibilities, but that job increased my self-reliance, and I was proud that my bosses saw something in me. They seemed to have plans for the young Black girl on the fourteenth floor.

Hard work and stifled grief. How the years blurred.

I turned thirty.

I sat on a yellow school bus with my pajamas in a backpack.

I'd been expecting a Greyhound bus, or one of those buses you see headed to Atlantic City, but, okay, this will do. It was cold outside and we'd left New York City behind. My best friend, Amanda, had given me the gift of a weekend retreat at the Sivananda Ashram in the Catskills. I was living in Brooklyn, which meant an early morning subway ride to 23rd street in Manhattan, where I was supposed to meet the bus and the rest of the group who wanted a break from the city, for an 8 a.m. departure. I was excited for my thirtieth birthday, but I was asking some big questions, too. I worked all the time, and I was getting tired of the stress. I knew I needed something new in my life. I wanted to be a little more free-spirited, and less tied down to a nine-to-five job.

Sleep-away camp was something I'd always wanted to do as a kid in Florida, and I thought this weekend away might scratch that itch. Along with my pajamas, I also had Paulo Coelho's *The Alchemist,* a journal, a change of clothes, and a bathing suit. I was planning on figuring out the future while sitting in the sauna.

The bus ride. I'm a flutter of nerves. I didn't know what to expect. It made the two-and-a-half-hour drive north feel like I was starting a new school year. I'm not a religious person, but I'd always been curious about meditation, and I wondered what it would feel like. We arrived at the temple, which was painted a rich red with white trim. The main house had stairs leading up to the entrance, and the sleeping quarters were in the back. Everything was tranquil and stunningly beautiful.

The silence was what I noticed first. If New York City is the place that never sleeps, this is the place that always sleeps and dreams.

I put my backpack in the small, unadorned room that I would be sharing, and I explored the property. The main building was surrounded by forest—mostly evergreens stretching way up into the sky. The deeper I went into the trees, the more I realized how terrified I was. I remember saying to myself, *You are such a city girl.* Give me a busy NYC street and I know how to behave. I know when to smile and when to pull back my shoulders to look bigger, tougher. I didn't know what to do in the forest. I was imagining getting lost. Bears and cougars. And that silence. The silence was overwhelming. I found myself thinking of my mum and death. It's hard not to sound simplistic with questions like where do we go when we die. But, where do we go when we die? Every thought was weightier in the woods.

I felt close to her, as if being in an unknown place allowed me to open up to her. I missed her voice. The temple bells brought back the sound of her bangles jangling when she opened the front door. The fresh, green air carried the scent of thyme, pimento seeds, and curry. Chicken marinating in the fridge in the red bowl.

I gave myself permission to think of her, sorrow and all.

Saturday was centred on a sweat lodge, facilitated by a leader from an Indigenous community from the region. He had a strong voice and kind eyes, and he explained how heat was used to purify the mind, body, and soul. His people used the sweat lodge when seeking wisdom, and to heal from trauma.

We were invited into a small dome made of sticks, stones, and animal hides. It was damp and muddy, and as the radiant heat hit me, my skin felt like it was on fire. I inhaled hot, moist air and closed my eyes. An elder sat at the centre of the dome. He reminded us to breathe. Be calm. Focus on something you love. I panicked a couple of times because everything felt too close and too intense, but I remained still and tried to breathe. As time passed, I felt like I was outside my body. Hearing everything, and nothing. I could smell everything, and nothing. I could touch everything, and nothing. It was like a dream, and at the very end, my mother was next to me holding my hand. Her fingers were soft and alive, and she squeezed my hand before she was gone.

I lasted thirty minutes in the tent, but it felt like hours. I dragged my exhausted, dehydrated body outside into the cool air. Surrender. Surrendering to something bigger than myself. I lay on the ground outside the tent under the starry black sky feeling every cell in my body. There's such a relief in crying.

There in the trees, away from the city.

How can a single weekend change everything?

Mealtime at the ashram was transformative. We ate in silence, and with nothing to distract from the food, each bite became important. I actually *tasted* the food in a way that felt different. I wasn't mindlessly eating to fill my stomach, I was chewing every morsel and accepting it into my body.

The food was simple and vegan—dishes like homemade tofu in broth, steamed dal with fennel seeds, and sea-salted quinoa. Many of the vegetables (carrots, celery, cauliflower) were harvested from the ashram's garden. The way the vegetables were honoured and used in dishes amounted to a ceremony. Food wasn't *just* to eat, it was to connect with the earth, the seasons, and the sun.

On Sunday morning, I had the opportunity to volunteer in the kitchen—the only space where guests were allowed to talk freely. Working at MTV, I had disconnected from food. I rarely cooked for myself, and when I did, it was generally something easy like a stir-fry and rice, or pasta and sauce. Here was an opportunity to share the task of creating a meal for all the guests.

The ashram's kitchen was humble and clean—cupboards filled with simple off-white plates and bowls. Glasses were small tumblers, cutlery was basic silverware. The counters were melamine and the chopping boards well-loved slabs of wood.

The cook showed me how to make a spice blend with cumin seeds, coriander, fennel, and some other whole spices. We cooked mung beans and lentils—beans that I didn't grow up eating. We made brown rice, too. Being Jamaican, I knew how to make parboiled white rice. I came out of the womb knowing how to do that. But I'd never made brown rice. Not once.

In that temple kitchen, I was invited to cook with intention. Think about what you make, every ingredient, know your place, be humble and open, understand that you are part of the chain that grew this food, that needs this food. Everything grows and passes away, but there is meaning, joy, and colour to be found on that journey. If you put consciousness into how you eat and how you cook, the food will reflect your thoughts. Some kind of beautiful symbiosis takes place, where the ingredients become your wishes and help your wishes come true. I had learned something similar from the Rastafarian community in Atlanta, but there in the ashram kitchen I was feeling the spiritual side in an even deeper way.

Open, trying to be humble, I realized what a loss I felt, longing for love, longing for home. I realized how deeply sad I was.

When that yellow school bus pulled back into Manhattan, I knew I wanted to be a chef.

Back to Brooklyn on Sunday night, still buzzing from the trees and the food. As soon as I walked in the door, I started researching culinary schools. That week on Friday, I attended an open house at the Natural Gourmet Institute on 21st Street. A culinary school that focused mostly on vegetarian cuisine, NGI offered a two-year part-time program, and the whole vibe felt right to me. Up the elevator in the 150-year-old Manhattan building, doors opened onto the welcome desk where Denise greeted me. It had a family-like feel. New wood finishes made the place shine, and the classrooms were spotless.

I knew it would be a stretch financially, but I also knew it was what I needed to do. In my entrance interview, I talked about my mum, about her cancer, and about how deeply I wanted to know more about foods that healed. I was accepted into the school, which meant I had to find the tuition. I knew I couldn't afford the whole thing, but I dreaded asking my dad for help.

It was a difficult phone call. I'd been financially independent for many years, and I didn't want to become entangled in my dad's ideas of job security and risk. I didn't want to fight with him or to explain how I knew that I needed to become a chef.

Maybe if I worked full-time while doing the part-time program, I could afford to do it. But I still needed the tuition up front. I smoked a little pot to relax, but I was fired up. I wanted this to happen.

"Daddy, can I talk to you about something?" He already knew. "How much do you need?"

Eighteen thousand dollars. It included everything, all uniforms and supplies. It was a lot of money, but I promised to pay him back. He asked how I could possibly leave my well-paying job at MTV. *What kind of a future will you have as a cook?* He even called the school to speak with the post-graduate counsellor. He asked about jobs and placements for students.

And then he actually said yes. It was a stretch for him, a huge sacrifice. He really set it up for me. He believed in me even if he didn't know what kind of job I'd have at the end of it all.

NGI was a special place. The school was established back in the late seventies by an Argentine woman named Annemarie Colbin. She was a modern pioneer in conceptualizing food as medicine. She believed that food should be whole, fresh, local, seasonal, traditional, balanced, and delicious. The size of the school was perfect, not too big, lots of personal attention.

I knew I didn't want to go to a traditional culinary school. The Culinary Institute of America and the International Culinary Center were the big-name schools in New York at the time, and I thought about them, but soon realized that I didn't want to join the military—the culinary brigade. I wanted small classes and a more relaxed vibe. I was up for a challenge, but I didn't want to be broken down by instructors so they could build me back up into some perfect replica of themselves. I knew little about the food and beverage industry, but I knew enough about myself to want to be respected and appreciated, not to be humiliated. I wanted something different.

I'm sure that mentality has changed over the past few years, as much-needed attention has been brought to the fucked-up power dynamics in culinary schools and professional kitchens throughout the world. I'm glad I made the choice that I did to go to NGI. Definitely challenging, but humane as well.

On two floors of that historic building I learned how to cook. We focused on vegetarian food, but also did classes on the butchery of finfish and chicken. I learned how to brunoise carrots, celery, leeks. First julienne, then turn a quarter turn and dice. I learned how to make the five mother sauces in French cuisine: béchamel, velouté, espagnole, hollandaise, and tomato. I learned other French techniques and Japanese knife skills, and I learned how to work as a team with other chefs, divide the work, and understand every part of the process. We had classes on veganism, Ayurvedic medicine, and whole foods. How to source the best ingredients and how important it is to know where your food is coming from. These are all things that have made me the chef and restaurant owner I am today.

One of my favourite classes was baking. The upstairs classroom housed the muffin tins, springform pans, bread loaf pans, candy thermometers, cookie sheets, and a variety of quiche pans.

"Okay class, who likes cookies?" Sheepishly, every hand reached for the ceiling.

"We're going to transform classic chocolate chip cookies today. We're going to make them all-natural." Welcome to the fundamentals of alternative baking. There was a low murmur in the classroom. I overheard someone say, "We're going to be here forever."

The objective was to create a batch of cookies that were vegan, gluten-free, nut-free, and sugar-free. It was a unique opportunity. I've always loved making cookies, but watching those classic ingredients transformed into a healthy cookie was dope. Move over, all-purpose flour and meet an unbleached gluten-free flour blend. Instead of eggs, we used applesauce or one tablespoon of flax meal and three tablespoons of water. Chocolate chips became carob chips. No white sugar, only brown rice syrup. Last but not least, we ditched the butter for unprocessed coconut oil. It was transformative. It made me understand the importance of inclusive options for potential clients. Learning how to create texture and flavour. We were shown how to make a damn good cookie without the traditional ingredients. A treat my diabetic father could enjoy without worry. It was profound.

Some of the biggest names in the vegetarian and vegan food industry were trained at the institute, like vegan culinary icon and restaurateur Amanda Cohen, and cookbook author and James Beard Award–winning chef Bryant Terry.

Demo classes were opportunities for us to put all of our learning into practice. Chef Rich made a class into a student battle where we were given one ingredient, and we had to make some kind of wicked dish from it. In one battle, I had cauliflower, and although I was nervous as hell, I made a delicious lasagna with the cauliflower and nutritional yeast. I didn't win, but Chef Rich thought the dish was creative and tasty, and when you're at school, just that little bit of encouragement can mean so much.

All the classes we took, demos we performed, and books we read were preparing us for our final dinner. We were asked to create a multi-course menu—to develop the recipes, write the menu, order the ingredients, buy the flowers, set the tables, and invite friends and family to partake. Our particular group offered a three-course vegan feast celebrating Africa. The four of us had spent the past several months together cooking, eating, learning, yearning for this night and, here it was, our ode to the African continent. We worked as a small brigade to research the spices of the continent, and we were ready to create our own spin on traditional dishes with the utmost respect for the food and cultures we were celebrating. We made a peanut salad with oranges, berbere spiced stew, and a hibiscus dessert that our guests loved.

That was the first meal I made as a newly minted chef, and it felt so good. I was proud of myself and my team, and seeing the enjoyment on our guests' faces was addictive. I wanted to do it again right away, to feed people good food that made their insides hum.

In the last few weeks of my time at NGI, I saw a poster on a bulletin board asking for volunteers at the James Beard House on 12th Street West. I didn't know much about the James Beard House, but I knew I wanted more experience, and to meet other people interested in cooking, so I applied.

Walking into Beard House was like entering your grandma's house—the decor was dated, and it smelled like mothballs, slow-cooked meats, and a dish of holiday candies. There were runners covering holes in the carpet.

The stains and water-damaged ceiling belied the importance of this place, although the posters on the walls gave a hint of it. This house changed the conversation around food and food preparation in America. James Beard, who was anointed the "Dean of American cookery," was a pioneer foodie, an early champion of local products and markets. He nurtured a generation of American chefs and cookbook authors who altered the way we eat. It was all pretty exciting to me.

My first volunteer experience was to help with a dinner cooked by Chef Beverly Gannon. The fact that she was from Hawaii interested me, as I was working to secure my NGI-required externship at a restaurant in Kauai. At that point in my career, I knew little about Gannon—an absolute powerhouse of a woman. I was inexperienced and hella nervous—still in culinary school, after all.

The kitchen team was made up of Black and Brown line cooks and dishwashers, some experienced and some not at all. The faces that made up the back of the house were the real James Beard House, the people who kept the place running smoothly although they were rarely seen. For some of the staff, working in kitchens was the only job that was possible for them because English was their second or third language. This is such a common story, such a common sight in restaurants throughout North America: the distinction between front of house and back of house being drawn along racial lines.

Although I was nervous, I felt safe in that kitchen. I felt connected, like I was working with my brothers. They all had a story about how they ended up at Beard House. I'm pretty sure they saw me as terrified but eager, and a little aloof (play it cool whenever possible; don't let them see you sweat). I tried to show off the skills I'd learned over the time I spent at NGI.

Any of these men could have been my father when he first left Jamaica.

My dad was skeptical about me becoming a chef. I think a big part of that had to do with job security, but just as importantly, it had to do with racism within the service industry. He didn't want his little girl to be "the help." He didn't want me to spend my life serving people who didn't see me.

I looked around that kitchen and felt both comforted and disheartened. These people who made up the Beard kitchen would probably never be seen or thanked or appreciated in the way they should be. They would never dine in the room as guests. They wouldn't make the same tips as the people who worked the front of the house. Working in the back of the house, we never did. It seemed deeply unfair. I hoped one day that I could do something to challenge that dynamic.

Chef Gannon created a menu that night that took her guests on a tour of Hawaii through the eyes of a Jewish, Texas-born chef. The menu influenced many of the dishes at my first restaurant, Saturday Dinette, and it still influences me today. To express my love for many different cuisines on one plate can be both exciting and delicious. It can challenge expectations and celebrate diversity. To combine Hawaiian ingredients with Jewish preparations and Texan flair was a revelation. For me, the list of dishes from that night is like a perfectly paced poem. From hors d'oeuvres like curried lobster wontons with mango-plum sauce, to mains of crispy skin Big Island amberjack with coconut curry sauce, to the final sweet course of passion fruit crème brûlée with macadamia nut tuile, Chef Gannon created a mind-blowing combination of flavourful dishes that worked perfectly together.

At the end of the night when the volunteers were standing around eating the leftovers, I had a chance to tell Chef Gannon that I'd be graduating soon and I was hoping to do my externship in Kauai. My only connection to Hawaii was my mum's great desire to see the islands. I heard Mummy and one of her dear friends, Auntie Myrna, talking about wanting to visit beautiful, mighty places, and they both agreed that Hawaii would check both of those boxes.

Chef Gannon said, "Well, once your externship is complete, look me up on Maui."

Come on, that was a job offer right? Ha! Well, for me, that's exactly what I heard, so I began to plot, plan, and find a way to get to Maui from Kauai. If the universe gives you opportunities, don't let them slip away. Act quickly, and you'd better be ready.

Witnessing Chef Gannon in the kitchen that night allowed me to glimpse what might be possible for me if I worked hard in this industry. I was both motivated and uncertain. I questioned my abilities. I can put on a good face (you know, never let them see you sweat and all that), but there are days when I wonder if a dish is going to work, if the ingredients I'm using will lead to the best combination of flavours possible. Difficult days can lead to self-sabotage, and to second-guessing myself. To wonder if I've done enough to deserve a chance to show my love of food.

That night, I stood in one of the most distinguished food establishments in NYC and dreamed that one day I'd come back to cook a meal for my peers. I'd celebrate all the people working in the kitchen, and I'd cook from my soul and share the story of how I came to make my own menu into a mouth-watering poem. That really would be a dream come true.

The externship (or *stage*) that most culinary schools require students to do looks a lot like a job in a kitchen, except you don't get a paycheque. There are stories of young chefs doing intense, scream-at-you-until-you-get-it-right trial-by-fire externships in all kinds of fine dining restaurants. Your stereotypical military-type kitchen where a—generally—white dude in a tall white hat yells until he's red in the face. If you make it through, you're a sur-vivor. And if you crack, it can be the end of your career. It can be a tough place for many new cooks, and in the white male–dominated world of kitchen culture, it can be even tougher for Black and Brown women.

My externship, on the other hand, was both relaxed and inspir-ing.

The Natural Gourmet Institute was a well-established school with a great reputation, and many alumni had gone on to do impressive things across the country. A variety of vegan and vegetable-forward cafés, restaurants, bakeries, delis, markets, and catering companies had been opened by NGI graduates, and when I was trying to figure out where I wanted to do my externship, I knew my credentials would make me a desirable candidate. In a comprehensive list of vegan res-taurants in the United States, I happened upon Blossoming Lotus, the one furthest from New York City, the one located on the east coast of the island of Kauai.

At the time I didn't know that when Blossoming Lotus first opened, it was a cutting-edge, incredibly popular vegan restaurant frequented by stars like Woody Harrelson and Demi Moore. I just knew that it was on one of the Hawaiian Islands, and that was good enough for me.

Opened in 2002 by Bo Rinaldi and Chef Mark Reinfeld, the res-taurant was defying the idea that vegan cuisine was simple and boring. Vegetarian and vegan cuisines up until that point were often thought of as "hippie food." Nut loaves of lentils and walnuts, scrambled tofu with turmeric and nutritional yeast, chunky stews with root vegetables and beans. All delicious, of course, but quite simple. Frances Moore Lappé's 1971 best-seller, *Diet for a Small Planet*, had opened many people's eyes to the negative environ-mental impact of meat production, as well as the possibility of feeding more of the world's residents with a vegetarian diet. Becoming vegetarian became a political decision, and in some ways politics outweighed the actual food being created.

Chef Reinfeld made dishes that were complex and layered, that challenged your taste buds and your mind. He gave vegan food its own identity and proved that flavour can come from many different sources, not just animal products.

I applied to the restaurant and I was accepted. I left cold, grim New York City in January, and flew west to the most northern of the Hawaiian Islands, the one they call the "Garden Island." Kauai is a thousand shades of green.

Walking out of the airport I was breathless with excitement. The warm air tasted like salt water, and the sky was that tropical blue that seems impossible in photos. On the bus into town, I couldn't stop smiling. Lush mountains stretched out beside me, and the water looked like liquid jewels.

I couldn't afford to stay in a hotel for six weeks, so I'd booked a bed at a surfers' hostel a short walk away from Blossoming Lotus. The hostel smelled of stale beer, suntan lotion, and surfboard wax. The "walls" between beds in the co-ed dorm were made of old, ratty sheets.

This was nothing like my suburban, Floridian upbringing, but my experiences in New York were a little more comparable, and living in that city had thickened my skin. It made me more alert, and cautious of my surroundings. I'm generally pretty laid-back, but as a Black woman moving through the world, I've learned to always protect my neck.

My alarm set for 6 a.m., I went to bed early that night, excited for my first day at the restaurant. It took me a while to fall asleep in the strange new space, but it was quieter than my Brooklyn apartment, and the warm stillness finally worked its magic.

Unfortunately, I was woken up at 3 a.m. by the sound of breaking glass, and then a heavy weight falling through the "wall" right on top of me. Half-asleep, but muscles twitching with adrenalin, I started screaming and kicking at whatever had just landed on me. I found myself punching a drunk girl and her boyfriend who hadn't made it back for the midnight curfew. While I screamed at them, they told me to relax, it was an accident, and then all the lights in the hostel were on, the cops were called, and they were removed from the dorm. My first night in Hawaii was fucked! I did finally go back to sleep, but in the morning, I found a new hostel.

That morning, for a while, I stood in front of the mirror in the hostel's tiny washroom, and my smile disappeared. I wondered if I was crazy for doing this. I knew no one, and I had no idea what I was getting myself into. I had left a solid job at MTV and the familiarity of NYC, where I was getting to know the culinary world in a deeper way.

At the time I was dating a university professor named Marty. He had quite an intellect. His expertise was in Caribbean and Latin American studies, post-colonialism, and the African Diaspora. We met one night, dancing, at a club in Brooklyn. He was from Trinidad, a father of one. He promised to come and join me on Maui at the tail end of my trip. I looked forward to travelling with him, but I was also ready for a break from some of the pressure of dating someone so book-smart. I was constantly measuring my own intellect against the intellects of the women he had dated previously. It made me insecure.

There's a dark pool of doubt in me. Every adventure I've been on, this insecure side of me starts wandering up my spine, waking me up, catching me in the mirror. As I said, I don't sit still much, and when I do, because I do . . . maybe that's when doubt creeps in. And at those times, almost as a way to make myself sit still, I tell myself the worst things—as if it makes my reality feel more real. I did that then, and I do it now. *I don't deserve to be here, I'm going to be a terrible cook. I'm a fool for leaving things behind. I'm alone on an island at dawn, and I've never worked in a restaurant.*

But every adventure is exactly that. Something new. A challenge. Fruit hanging low or high, I want it. I am not afraid of working until it hurts. This was me carving my path. Right? This is me always trying to carve my path.

I changed into my houndstooth pants, a white T-shirt, and my chef shoes. I washed my face and brushed my teeth, I grabbed my knife roll, and I walked out into the green world.

Little Dragon's hypnotic song "Scribbled Paper" in my headphones,

I walked along the gravel shoulder of the main road toward the restaurant, and I smiled again. The sky was an incredible kaleidoscope of blue, orange, red, and purple.

I had two restaurant jobs in Hawaii. This first at Blossoming Lotus taught me about ingredients. For all my anxiety about how I would do, the reality of Blossoming Lotus was that it was incredibly relaxed. In many ways it was not what I had expected.

The restaurant was in the centre of a beachside community called Kapa'a, tucked away in the back of a mini-mall. The mall had an eighties vibe, with beige clapboard buildings and simple wooden signs: Key Cutting, Office Space for Rent, Nail Salon. Above Lotus was a flooring company, and right beside it was a beach shop that sold floaties, towels, knick-knacks, and aloha shirts.

I was on time, which, for me, means fifteen minutes before my shift starts, and I was anxious. I found myself in a quaint dining area with rattan chairs, wooden tables, and benches covered with seafoam-green fabric. Walls of windows invited a flood of natural light. I asked for the chef, and the host pointed through a second dining area toward the kitchen. The restaurant was much larger than I imagined—it seated about a hundred people. In its heyday, the kitchen would have been frenetic, calls for Bombia Enchilada and Mighty Aphrodite's Greek Salad would have filled the air, and dishes would have left the pass like clockwork. By the time I arrived, though, the decor felt a little dated, the seat covers were faded and a little dirty, and the busyness had slowed to a relaxed pace—Lotus was slow and tranquil.

Chef Reinfeld, who had opened the restaurant, was no longer in the kitchen day to day, and the sous-chef, Ryan, had taken over. Blossoming Lotus had other locations in Portland, Oregon, and they had planned to open one in California. When I arrived in Kapa'a, Chef Reinfeld no longer needed to be there. His recipes were set, and people knew what to expect, so he managed from afar.

The staff was small, and everyone looked a little tired that day. Uniforms were kind of old, top button undone, aprons had been washed way too many times. I think they'd all been used to a faster-paced kitchen, and sometimes you feel most tired when you're able to slow down and think.

Like the rest of the restaurant, the kitchen needed a deep clean, but it was totally serviceable and I felt comfortable from the get-go. Double swinging doors linked the kitchen to the dining room, there was lots of counter space, and cushy mats on the floor gave some relief to weary legs. The most impressive part of the space was a big metal shelving unit with infinite jars of organic hemp seeds, pepita seeds, chia seeds, flaxseeds, brown rice, mung beans, chickpeas, lentils, macadamia nuts, Brazil nuts, cashews; every legume, grain, nut, and seed you could ever want. They had spared no expense to keep this collection of the best ingredients well stocked. It was a vegan's dream kitchen, and the ingredients were turned into delicious, boundary-pushing dishes.

I bellied up to the long stainless-steel counter where I started right into lunch prep with the two other cooks. They were both from the mainland, and I was interested to know how they ended up in Kauai. They said the island was a hard place to leave.

Kauai got into my blood. Hands down it was the most beautiful place I'd ever been.

Everywhere I looked, there were massive plants and trees that dripped green. Rubber plants, palm trees, and thick ferns. The island is 97 percent undeveloped mountain ranges and rainforests, and I started to understand Kauai as the island people who want seclusion and raw, untouched natural beauty visit.

The early morning sun on my skin made me think of mornings in Florida, but, even more deeply, it made me feel that trip I took with Mummy and Tanya to visit our cousins in Jamaica. There was a similarity to the green of the mountains, the wild, untouched, oversized palms, and the hot jungle. There was something familiar about it, and it gave me comfort.

Kauai didn't feel like the tourist-centred version of Hawaii that

I was expecting. The small historic beachside community of Kapa'a was traditional and unspoiled. Blossoming Lotus brought a lot of visitors to town and helped support other local businesses as a result, but Kapa'a never experienced any profound gentrification because of its location on the sleepy island.

The first thing I learned to make was roasted pepita seeds, served as a welcoming dish at each table. The seeds were plump and the colour of pale jade, and I learned how to flavour them with agave syrup, tamari, and toasted, ground fennel seeds. They were delicious and totally addictive, and I still make them today. Versions of two other dishes that I learned to make at Lotus have also appeared frequently on my subsequent menus: summer rolls and a nine-layer enchilada dish. The summer rolls were these bountiful bouquets of crisp lettuce, rice noodles, shiny red peppers, carrots, mint, and Thai basil, all wrapped in rice paper. We made them assembly-line style, and I was schooled in the art of working with rice paper.

My first few were clunky, loosely wrapped rolls that we kept in the kitchen for staff. They would never see a guest. I kept trying, and when I got the hang of it, I could manipulate the delicate rice paper without tearing it.

Dunk the paper in hot water.

Hydration is key.

Fill it with the flavours and colours you want.

The paper sticks to the stainless-steel countertop.

This is like rolling a joint.

Tight, but not too tight.

Eventually my rolls were like bouquets of flowers wrapped in paper. The gorgeous vegetables inside were the blooms that the rice paper kept hidden until you took a bite. I learned to work quickly. None of the chefs liked making summer rolls because they were super labour-intensive, so it was a job I was asked to do almost every day. By the end of my six weeks at Lotus, I was totally done with them. It took me a couple of years to rekindle my appreciation for them!

I started my day shift at 8 a.m. or my evening shift at 3 p.m. I had a coffee, then set up my mise en place—all the ingredients as well as the equipment I'd need to make whatever Chef Ryan needed. I'd have my two side towels, my sharpened knives, and all my washed ingredients right in front of me. I never worked the line at Lotus—I only did prep—but I did have the opportunity to watch the line, and I saw what that dance looks like. Forward step with the left foot. Watch your colleague's toes. Right foot steps sideways to the right. Someone calls *behind!* or *hot!*, and they both shuffle and bend. Busier kitchens were in my future, but I still learned that to work well together, staff have to be connected and in sync. When the line works, it's a beautiful thing.

I was the only woman in the Lotus kitchen, and being a little older gave me a bit of a motherly presence. Everyone treated me with respect. I brought energy into a kitchen that wasn't overly enthusiastic, and people appreciated that. My confidence didn't come from my culinary experience, obviously, as I didn't have any. It came from my discipline, my willingness to work hard, and a desire to learn.

Because of my hard work, I was given more responsibility and started prepping more difficult recipes and learning more dishes. I learned the importance of a chef's mise en place, as well as how to limit food waste and keep food cost within budget. I learned the acronym FIFO: first in, first out. Older food is found at the front of the fridge so that it's used before the newer ingredients are used—important stuff when you're running a restaurant. My brain was full of new, crucial information, and I loved the feeling. And at Blossoming Lotus, no one yelled at me. I was respected, and when you're respected you want to respect others. My *stage* made me recognize that respect is everything in the kitchen, and I'm so grateful for that. It has informed every kitchen I've worked in and run ever since. It's not just ingredients that make a restaurant kitchen, it's staffing and how the staff interact. Luckily for me, I worked with good staff *and* great ingredients.

Building flavour is the key to developing any delicious dish. It's obvious when you think about it, but it wasn't always foremost in my mind when I was starting out. Now, I think about sweet notes crystallizing. Salty bits quenching thirst. Sourness puckering the lips. Spicy heat tingling the tongue. Umami blending it all together.

Growing up, my mum cooked rice with coconut milk, scallions, and Scotch bonnet peppers. She understood the technique of making rice, and then she built layers of flavour to make that rice even more interesting. At Lotus we used rice, but we also used quinoa, wheat berries, barley, and couscous. And I tasted the results when they were cooked in a flavourful liquid, infusing the grains as they cooked. Each dish at Lotus was created with that idea of layering flavours.

The nine-layer enchilada dish totally blew my mind. Creamy beans and vegan cheese made from cashews, fresh vegetables and tofu and nutritional yeast, vibrant herbs, red pepper flakes, spelt tortillas, tahini, and olives. It defied my idea of how complex a vegan dish could be.

Complexity was never a fear for me, and there is always this challenge with vegetarian and vegan cooking to go deeper and more complex than regular cooking. Some sort of requirement to prove yourself, that you're just as good as the others. It bothered me as a way of thinking, and it reminded me of what it's like sometimes to be a Black woman, having to prove yourself more than others in this industry. But I was up for the challenge.

I've come out the other side of that now, later in life, confident in simplicity—finding the beauty in simple ingredients. But if Lotus at that time was a bit too focused on complex vegetarian dishes, it at least taught me how to work with those ingredients— how to play with fireworks if fireworks were needed. It fostered creativity, imagination, and fancy.

Early in my externship, on a day when the restaurant was closed, Chef Ryan took me to a farm that supplied our field lettuces. It was a total revelation to me that lettuce was one of the *only* local items on the menu at Blossoming Lotus. On this lush island of abundant growth, how had they reached the conclusion that it was less expensive to source products from California, Japan, and elsewhere?

Kauai is about 1,500 square kilometres, which isn't a whole lot of space, and if you take into consideration how much of the island is mountain ranges and rainforest, it doesn't leave a lot of room for crops. Add to that the fact that farmers were being pushed off their land by big chemical companies who were able to test their products on crops all year round because of the long growing season, and you can understand how Lotus had to source products off island. For years, residents have been protesting against the use of the chemical companies' poisonous substances. They worry about what's in their water, air, and crops. It still seems like a tragedy to me that in such a fertile place, farmers can't safely grow everything they need, and folks can't easily get access to local, nutritious food.

In Ryan's dirty old pickup truck, no seatbelt on, my arm hanging out the open window, I had my first long look at the rest of the island. He seemed more comfortable outside in his flip-flops than he did in the restaurant. Travelling those roads with him, I really got a sense of someone who loved food but had lost his love of preparing it. Not having the freedom to create your own menu can do that. This industry can burn you out. Most industries can. Once you lose your creative expression—because you have to, because you're part of a bigger team, because you have investors and other interests telling you what to do—you lose that inner spark. Most cooks at restaurants reach a point where they want to make their own mark, add their own flavours to the prestige of the place. And if you can't, if all you can do is master technique, pay meticulous attention to other people's creations, over and over . . . It's good if you can remember the love that set you down this path.

From the paved road onto a country road of tire tracks with a mound of green grass in between, we arrived at the farm. We pulled up alongside a plowed field covered in hoop houses, containing lettuces of every colour. The field was surrounded by palm and banana trees, and the soil on the edge of the growing patch was red from bauxite.

The farmer came out to meet us and asked if I'd like a tour. We walked between the rows of vibrant lettuces, and he pointed out specific varietals. When I said I knew absolutely nothing about farming, he explained his process of harvesting and then tilling the lettuce roots back into the soil that he would then use to plant again. It seemed harmonious and circular, and I asked if that's what made his lettuces so freakin' good.

I was totally naive about the politics of food production, and I was really only concerned with learning how to become a better chef. I know it seems strange, but it hadn't hit me in a profound way that producers were the key to creating beautiful food in the kitchen. Now it's how I approach every dish I make, but at the time I was inexperienced and more concerned with my knife skills and cooking techniques. Being close to the land, listening to farmers, conjuring my ancestors, and learning about native fruits and their medicinal properties—it was all very different from being in a farmer's market in Brooklyn.

We stopped, and the farmer asked me to close my eyes as he gave me a taste of some mustard greens and romaine hearts. They were spicy and crisp, and I had a real sense of terroir when I ate them. I could smell the earth and taste the water that he had used to grow these leafy jewels. The smell of fresh morning dew was still present, and the field was quiet and calm. With my eyes closed, I tested myself. I tried to see if I could create a dish that would feature those tastes. Could I put the mustard greens in a bean stew? Would their spicy notes add the right flavour? Could I stir-fry them with tofu and mung beans? What kind of dressing would I put on the romaine? What kind of softness could I add to elevate the crunch? It's a special memory for me because it was my first real connection with a producer, and it showed me how important a chef's relationships can be with farmers and other growers.

The farmer had already harvested our order, and he handed us two huge bags full of different lettuces: shades of emerald, lime, seaweed, and forest, as well as orange, pink, and purple. It was the most beautiful collection I've ever seen.

After my six weeks at Blossoming Lotus, I travelled from Kauai to Maui where I was to spend a month at Chef Gannon's restaurant, the Hali'maile General Store. Remember, I had spoken to Chef Gannon from NYC after meeting her at the James Beard House dinner, and she had said, *Yes, you can come and work for me.* If Kauai is the sleepy island, Maui is like Disneyland or Atlantic City. It's busy and flashy and exciting. And it's breathtakingly beautiful, too.

Like the two islands, the kitchens were also very different. Chef Gannon's kitchen was intensely busy, and, if I thought I was nervous at Lotus . . . this was a different league. The line was frantic, and there was a full brigade of chefs working. The Hali'maile General Store was one of the most celebrated restaurants on the island. Chef Gannon's brand of fusion—which combined her love of Hawaiian cuisine and the Jewish comfort food she grew up with—was popular with tourists and locals, and the dining room itself was homey and relaxed. The entrance was a screened-in porch door, and just outside the door were rocking chairs where guests would sit and look out at the pineapple fields across the gravel driveway. I hitchhiked to work because the restaurant was "upcountry," the area on the east side of Maui away from the shoreline.

Apprehensive or not, I jumped in. Free labour is always appreciated. In a kitchen that busy, you can't expect people to explain things in detail, and I learned how to figure stuff out on my own.

Mashing potatoes was one of my first projects there. I had memories of mashing potatoes at home, Thanksgiving and Christmas, Mummy wanting them just so. Like everything in Hawaii, these potatoes were more colourful: purple, and the mash looked as pretty as morning glory flowers.

When people got used to my presence, I started supporting chefs on the grill, I continued with prep, and then I worked garde manger. Garde manger is the station where a chef prepares cold dishes such as salads, appetizers, canapés, and terrines. It's generally thought to be the gateway to other jobs on the line, but for me, in that restaurant, it was more than enough. The dish I made most often was an edamame hummus layered with crispy wonton skins and stacked with tuna sashimi. After one of the chefs showed me how to make it, I practiced assembling it before the restaurant opened.

What I learned at Hali'maile was that timing was everything. You've got to let people know when your dish will be ready and keep ahead of things—to work the line and not get worked by the line. Oh, and also, if a mouse runs between your feet while you're cooking, don't scream and yell "mouse!" No one—especially the guests—needs to hear that.

When my month at Hali'maile ended, Marty flew from NYC, and we spent a few days exploring the island together. I was excited to see him, but I was also interested to see if being in a totally different environment would ease some of my self-doubt.

He rented a car, and we drove the perimeter of Maui over the course of four days. Erykah Badu's album *Mama's Gun* was the soundtrack, and we blasted those songs over and over again. A lot of our connection was sexual, and we explored our bodies while we explored the island. I knew that our relationship wasn't going to last, and I knew my time in Hawaii was coming to an end, but I wanted to enjoy as much of both as I could.

We saw a young guy hitchhiking with a sign and a backpack, and I convinced Marty to pick him up. He was on his way home after getting supplies in town. When we arrived at his gravel driveway a few kilometres later, he asked if we wanted to come up to see where he lived with a bunch of other students and artists. I looked at Marty, and we both nodded. I always found myself curious about how people ended up in Hawaii and what their lives were like. We pulled up to the property, and it looked like a ghost town. There was no one else around and, of course, I started replaying scenes from horror films in my head. *Are we safe?* If I'd seen Jordan Peele's thriller *Get Out* back then, I never would have agreed to any of it! But I was with Marty, a tall, intuitive, muscular Trini with charm, and I was pretty sure nothing was going to happen.

The guy asked if we wanted to go see a waterfall and, again, we both said yes. Before that, though, he asked us to taste this fruit he called miracle fruit, and I'd never tasted anything like it. When you eat it, and then you eat something sour, it makes the sour food taste sweet. I know now that it originated in West Africa where it's used to sweeten palm wine and flavour other foods, but at the time I had no idea what the hell it was.

He led us through some trees, up some rocks, and when we arrived at a clearing, I could hear distant sounds that I didn't recognize. The guy looked at me and said, "Whales. They're mating." *Are you serious?*

You could see the joy in his face at showing these two New Yorkers this special place. "Come on."

Up some more rocks, another clearing, and then I saw them. Out there in the pristine blue of the Pacific were a dozen humpback whales, surfacing, shooting air from their blowholes, and vocalizing. I had another *Where am I?* moment, and then he was off again, saying we'd better get to the waterfall before high tide comes or we might get stuck. My internal alarm was whoop-whooping away, but we followed over some volcanic rocks, and then I slipped. Marty caught my arm just in time and pulled me up while I look down into a deep crevice. I would have died.

Marty stayed next to me as we kept going, and then, there it was. A waterfall scene to rival something from the Lord of the Rings series or *Avatar*. Tropical greenery cascading down volcanic rocks and a waterfall cut right in the middle. This unimaginably beautiful secret.

I like to think that somehow, somewhere in my belly, brain, or soul, these experiences in Hawaii found their way into my cooking. My love of surprise. The colours and the beauty taking me to unexpected places and conjuring some kind of *rapture*. That's what I felt looking at that waterfall. That's what I felt putting faith in a stranger and letting him take us to a place he wanted to show us. You take the adventure and see what happens.

Marty and the guy stripped naked and jumped into the pool below. I sat on a rock and watched. Got to take it all in.

What could be further from downtown traffic, people fighting, and the bass of car stereos? Strangers swimming naked and those sights, that calm. How can I capture that when I'm back in the city and cooking?

The culinary highlight of Marty's trip was eating at the Hali'maile. I'd told my co-workers about him, and they made us a super special meal. It's always illuminating to see a restaurant from the other side, and to experience the food as a guest, rather than a cook. I totally understood why people celebrated the Hali'maile. Each dish was a work of art that still managed to be comforting and approachable. At the end of our meal, the staff presented me with an envelope of money, explaining that they had been splitting tips with me without me knowing. It was unconventional to share tips with a *stagiaire* and I felt incredibly grateful. They had appreciated my hard work and wanted to reward me. After ten weeks without a paycheque, it was good to feel some green bills in my hand.

Hawaii is a bright light on my path to becoming a chef. So much learning and taking and giving. It sits big in my chest, formative, appreciated.

On our last night, I took Marty to Makena Beach in South Maui, a beach I'd gone to once with a woman I met at the restaurant. It was a wild place where people would go at sunset, and I wanted Marty to experience it. With music bumping, some people would strip down and dance naked, other people would juggle fire sticks, and some would be drumming, but everyone would start clapping when the sun started to set. At first, I didn't know what the hell they were doing. And then I felt this weird swell of gratitude. Everyone was thanking the sun for the day. Marty looked at me like, *What the fuck?*

"Just go with it," I told him.

# THREE

# WORK

One one coco full basket

Maybe it was a dream. Maybe it's all been a dream.

A man walked into my kitchen and said he wanted to help me. "That's the best meal I ever ate," he said. "I'd do anything for more of that. I'd do anything to help you put that on more plates."

Or something like that.

In my dream I made a dish, a curry chicken dish, that made this man so happy he offered to help me take hold of my future.

Imagine that. You set up a restaurant or you're cooking for a group of friends, and someone you've never met before is so taken by your food that he reaches into his wallet, the wallet of an angel, and showers you with money. Is that every cook's dream? It had to have been a dream.

People do love my curry chicken.

You know those moments in life where you can look back and say, *If I hadn't done that, this other thing wouldn't have happened?* You might not have met the love of your life if you hadn't gone out that night. You might not have been a success if you hadn't studied. Well, I wonder if I would have done anything I did over the last ten years if I hadn't made that curry chicken.

After Hawaii, I went back to Brooklyn and knocked on the door of a corner café in my neighbourhood called Tiny Cup. "I need a job."

Leslie hired me on the spot. I made desserts and cooked with gratitude. Food on the table. Coffee in my cup. And it was time to plan, to hustle.

On our last night together, Marty brought me to eat at a small family-run Senegalese restaurant called the Corner Bistro in Fort Greene. He knew that I'd love the food and thought maybe I could work there. We were still friendly, but we had drifted apart after Hawaii, and I didn't want a relationship to distract me from my new passion.

The lively restaurant with deep red walls was operated by the Dieng family. I called Abel, the owner and chef, the next day and asked for a job. I started a week later.

Abel fused West African flavours with French technique, and he became a mentor to me. I watched as he ran his family business with his wife and daughter. I saw them struggle and thrive, not knowing that years later I'd be doing the same thing. He was hard on me, and that was his way of showing me that he believed in me. He made me push myself, and he taught me how to make delicious food in a busy environment.

I became a member of the New York Women's Culinary Alliance, which allowed me to make connections with women in the industry who served as inspiration. Not just chefs, but food stylists, recipe developers, cookbook publishers—anyone interested in the broad world of food.

Hustling is imperative in that city. I was barely scraping by working at the Corner Bistro, and I needed to find other ways to make money. And, besides, I still wanted to learn everything. Maybe food styling could be fun. Before I worked at MTV, I was a wardrobe stylist. I worked in the wardrobe department on *Bad Boys II* and countless music videos from the late nineties—112,

Sisqó, Missy Elliott, Whitney Houston, Baha Men, Trick Daddy, as well as B-grade television shows like *Killer Flood*, and a Luther Campbell movie, too. I knew what looked good, and I thought I could make food look good, as well.

I learned about Michelle Dowell, a food stylist who worked on a whole range of publications, from cookbooks by Martha Stewart and the Barefoot Contessa, to magazines like *Bon Appétit* and *Food and Wine*. She was well known, and I liked her style.

I called her, emailed her, bugged her, and we eventually set up a time to meet at a New York Women's Culinary Alliance event. She didn't show up, but I didn't give up. I knew if she met me, she'd hire me. Eventually she said, "Fine, I'll meet with you! You are persistent," Ha ha. I can laugh now, but I'm not sure I'd be where I am today if I hadn't been so determined.

Michelle was a true master of her craft. She was a lone wolf, but for the bigger jobs, she needed a trusted assistant, and I eventually became that person for her. I think she appreciated my work ethic, my attention to detail, and the fact that I was hungry and always available. The money was decent, and I wanted to learn everything I could about styling, to train my eye and broaden my work experiences in the trade.

Michelle and I worked with a number of well-known celebrity chefs, but my favourite experience was with Bobby Flay at his home in the Hamptons. Bobby loved hip-hop, and to get him ready for any shoot, his assistant would put on something to amp him up. Wu-Tang Clan was on the playlist for today, and from *Enter the Wu-Tang (36 Chambers)* "Wu-Tang Clan Ain't Nuthin' ta F' Wit" started loud. It was as if we were at a WWF fight, lights dimmed waiting for the main event to start. I was cleaning up our work area, and I stopped to look for Michelle. I was totally caught off guard when this ginger-headed guy bobbing up and down walked out ready to turn it on. I loved every moment of it. Bobby Flay was badass. I got to see different sides of people working in their houses as a stylist. There was a different dynamic, and the intimacy was real.

It was through Michelle that I caught wind of a South African family who needed a private chef in the Hamptons. Before they committed, though, they wanted an opportunity to taste the chef's food, and that's how I found myself walking into a bright, airy loft in Tribeca with Chris, a friend and sous-chef extraordinaire, my palms sweaty and a recipe in my head. They seemed to be liberal expats, New York elite, downtown parents. The walls were lined with African-motif fabrics, sculptures, and a Basquiat original. There were African drums, and the soft earth tones of the motherland wrapped the couches and covered the windows.

Marissa met us at the door that Friday night, and she was immediately warm and open. On the phone a few days before, she had suggested I come and cook for her family and a few friends (twelve to fifteen people), and that meal would either lead to a summer job at their house in Bridgehampton, or not.

*Make a dish that means something.* I told myself that, and I settled on a version of the curry chicken that I'd grown up with. Instead of the dark meat that my mum always used, I used breast meat, which, in my experience, is a little more approachable in these settings. At our family dinner table in Plantation, we always used our hands, sucking the marrow from the bones, cracking the legs with our molars, and sucking any extra juices that hadn't been sopped up with the rice. But I never know how comfortable people are with that.

For me the dish was Jamaica on a plate. Saffron-yellow sand, heat, home, and comfort. Doesn't matter where I am, curry takes me to the same place. Nerves aside, I knew that I could share that feeling.

By that time, I had often cooked for strangers, but not in such a high-pressure environment. I remember a feeling of stage fright or being out of my comfort zone, on show to all of these white folks in the beautiful loft. When the chicken was finally ready, Chris and I loaded up platters, and the dish looked incredible—like mounds of glowing yellow diamonds. We made steamed rice, and we served naan from an Indian restaurant around the corner. There were pretty dishes full of garnishes—raita, cilantro, roasted cashews, coconut flakes, and mango chutney. We were back in the kitchen, cleaning up, and before they'd even finished eating, Marissa came in to say, "You're hired."

"Holy shit, Chris! We did it."

That was the first door that my curry chicken opened.

Knowing that I'd be living in the Hamptons five days a week, I gave my notice to Abel. He wasn't supportive of my decision, and neither was my dad. Abel said, "If you do this, you'll never be a chef." He didn't think that cooking for a family would allow me to hone my craft, and my dad had been skeptical of me stepping into a situation exactly like this.

"You're not the help. I don't want people looking down on you."

Cooking was what he knew, what he did back home in Jamaica. Hadn't he worked hard enough that his daughter didn't have to do this? Two important male figures in my life didn't want me to take the job—I had to prove them both wrong.

Marissa and her family treated me extremely well, and that first summer turned into two more. They always invited me to sit at the table with them for meals, and I almost felt like a part of their family. I also started cooking Shabbat dinner for them during the rest of the year when we were back in the city.

The Hamptons, east coast Long Island. It's two and a half hours from NYC, a beautiful place made up of both seaside and inland communities. In the summer, it's a popular playground for affluent New Yorkers. Secret beaches, quiet villages, breathtaking views, high-end restaurants, bars, and designer shops. Each village is quite different. Some are pretty relaxed, others scream excessive wealth, and still others are made of old money. I worked in Bridgehampton, which had a little of everything.

I shared a BMW X5 truck with the family's two nannies. I found back roads and pulled over to hear crickets and birds. Tried to avoid the high-traffic main roads to seek out trees and fields of flowers. So unlike Brooklyn. Serene and secluded. Small family farms sold blueberries, apples, and corn, which I bought by slipping a few dollars into a box. But also, obviously, there were signs of incredible wealth. Pristine golf courses and gated mansions.

The house we lived in that first summer was massive, a sprawling place that went on forever. It had white, vaulted ceilings, a fireplace, a large kitchen with wooden beams, and polished pebble-stone walls. Plenty of windows. A very different life. I remembered all my years scrambling for rent, apartments with no air conditioning. I cooked for the family all week, and then headed back to Brooklyn on the weekends, which kept me on solid ground. On Sunday night, I was back on the road.

Some people I knew in the city were impressed when I mentioned the Hamptons, as if I was actually a part of the Hampton set. It made me uncomfortable. I did make good money, but not *that* kind of money. I never felt like I actually belonged. And I wasn't meant to belong. Although there was no question I was appreciated, and I knew I played an important role for the family, it was my job.

My conversation with my dad was on my mind. I was cooking dinner for the family and Marissa's friends, also white South Africans. They had come from NYC to stay for a few days. The woman was named Denise, and I liked her immediately. She was stylish and very cool. In that kitchen in the Hamptons, though, Denise's husband approached me and said, "It's nice to see you in here. Reminds me of our maids in South Africa."

I didn't react. I got quiet. What did he say to me?

All of the oxygen had been removed from the room.

Later, though, I started crying. I wanted to walk away. My dad's worries kept coming back to me. Was he right? He warned me. How could I take money from these people? Do they all see me as a Black maid?

The internal dialogue was so loud, I called my friends to ask their thoughts, should I stay or should I go?

The money was good and it was my first private chef job. I have dreams bigger than you, man. Money and work. Work and money. I was struggling with my pride and his prejudice. I did my job, and I didn't pay him any heed. I didn't like him. I wasn't going to let him define me.

What I know about myself is I'm passionate about equal rights and abhor racism of any kind. I'm also a practical person and a good judge of character. Life isn't just about ideals, morality, and judgment; it's about you and me, real people, complicated needs, faces at a table. Marissa had been decent to me. They appreciated my food, they were otherwise respectful. You respect me, I respect you. Over time, I started cooking for Denise's family in the city, as well. When her husband was around, I'd square my shoulders and do my job. In my head I was never cooking for him, I was making food for Denise and her kids, and they loved every dish I made. I didn't avoid her husband, I just ignored him. He didn't deserve a thought in my head.

Nothing else was ever said to make me uncomfortable, and I knew if anything else ever rose up like that, I was out the door.

In the Hamptons I joined a gym so I could go somewhere kind of normal during my free time and get my sweat on. During other hours when I wasn't needed at the house, I headed to Sag Harbor, a little further north from Bridgehampton. It had a rich African American history that intrigued me.

From the late 1700s, Eastville, a neighbourhood on the outskirts of Sag Harbor, welcomed Black people who were formerly enslaved, and many worked as whalers and fishermen, or seamstresses and bakers. By 1840, Black people had built their own church in the area, and it's believed to have been a stop on the Underground Railroad. In the thirties, Maude Terry and her sister Amaza Lee Meredith bought a twenty-acre plot on reclaimed marshland in the area, and that was the beginning of one of the most enduring Black beach-front communities in the United States. It was a place where Black activism and innovation thrived, and people could live without the burden of systemic oppression.

B. Smith's was a popular restaurant in Sag Harbour. Smith, herself, was an incredibly influential Black restaurateur, TV personality, model, and businesswoman. She was a true icon, and her restaurant was a refuge for African Americans who lived near or were travelling in the Hamptons. She specialized in Southern soul food. That Low

Country food. Cajun. Creole. Dishes like crab cakes with remoulade, blackened catfish, corn cakes, and sweet tea.

Smith was hugely influential to me.

The first time I ate at her restaurant, she came out to the deck where I was watching the mid-summer sunset on the water. A familiar smile, open arms like my auntie offering me advice. "The crab cakes are my favourite . . . I've never seen you here before. You new to the area?" Her warm demeanour and voice encouraged me to drop my shoulders and exhale into the evening. If I needed to get away from work and its constant demands, I could escape to B.'s. Spending time at her restaurant was like refuelling. Like spending time with a good friend who understands you and leaves you feeling more alive. It's intense working as a personal chef, especially when you live with the family you work for. You're always at the office. But I was making good money, and I was becoming a more confident chef.

There's a Jamaican expression: One one coco full basket. You work hard, take one opportunity after another.

When I was at the restaurant, I felt like I was experiencing a celebration of Black food. I looked at B. and tried to imagine myself in her shoes one day. A very visible Black woman in an industry where people of colour are often made invisible. Crab cakes and a glass of bubbles, I toasted her.

Back in the city in September, I started cooking for both families, fully embracing the life of a private chef. I also worked for a young Russian family during the days, on Park Avenue, right across the street from Central Park, and right beside Trump Tower.

The next summer came, I went back to the Hamptons part-time. (Marissa had also hired a chef named David, and we split the season, one week on, one week off.) Brooklyn was still home, but I spent most of my time in other people's kitchens. I had money, but I had no life.

By the third summer with Marissa, David had become a bigger presence, and I was ready for a new adventure. I wasn't ready to give up the private chef life, though, and I wanted one client that I could focus on exclusively. My agent found me Patty and Mark.

They split their time between a condo in the Time Warner Building near Central Park, a house in the Hamptons, and a condo in Miami. It was a salaried position, and I was making 88K per year, plus a car, and I had a credit card that I could use to buy whatever ingredients I needed. They weren't all that curious about food. Patty was very particular about what she would eat. No nightshades. No spicy foods. Mark was a little bit more open. It was challenging in the beginning making separate menus for each of them, but I eventually found my rhythm. Every single day, every holiday, too.

It's a strange thing to be a central part of someone's life, but to ultimately feel like a feature on the wall. I think after a while, they didn't really see me at all. In some ways, I was like a part of the family—I was witness to their spats, their whims, their cravings, and their vices. While in the Hamptons, I would go downstairs, where my room was in the basement cut off from the rest of the house. I had a separate area that was my living room, with windows facing the outdoor storage area for chairs and tables. I was lonely. Isolated. I thought about quitting.

When they told me they'd purchased an apartment in Paris, I decided to stay with them a little longer, and I set out to learn French and to embrace the experience of being in France. I'd heard a story of my mum spending a weekend in Paris, a story without much content or detail, but I have a photo of her standing in front of the Eiffel Tower, and I began imagining her walking those streets, finding beauty in the architecture. Like I've said, my mum was artistic, but she rarely had the opportunity to exercise that part of herself. I think that was one of the things that made me sad about her going so early: her not having a chance to be more creative. I wished that she could have come to Paris with me. Just like I wished that she had been in Hawaii with me.

I recognized after she died how little I knew about her. At some level going to these places was a way of finding her, or at least looking for her.

Did she walk down the Champs-Élysées, like me, and yearn?

Patty and Mark rented a quaint apartment for me at 24 Rue Acacia, close enough to the building where they were living in the 7th Arrondissement. My apartment was on the ground floor, full of furniture from the seventies, with a kitchenette behind a plastic retractable wall. There was a hotplate, a small sink, a draining rack, and a fridge that was the perfect size for one. A wall unit held a TV, and I watched the French shows trying to learn the language. The closet door would bump into the front door, so I couldn't have both open at the same time.

I absolutely loved the space. It was tiny, quirky, and it reminded me of how little you need when the city around you is so beautiful. At least once a day I'd think, *I could happily live here forever.* The best part of the apartment was its private garden with a small rusty iron table, and a single chair. Roses climbed a low fence and there was a small patch of grass. It was magical.

When I wasn't working, I spent most of my days in the garden smoking a joint or a Gauloises cigarette. The woman who owned the apartment was in her eighties, and she was so elegant. So French. One night, in her Chanel suit and scarf, she took me to her favourite Chinese restaurant right around the corner.

I spent two months in Paris with Patty and Mark, and it was like a fairy tale. I had a French love affair, learned more of the language, and felt deeply connected to my mum, just by imagining her there with me every day.

Patty and Mark could be impulsive. Sometimes I was given an hour's notice that we were heading from NYC to Miami, or from Florida to the Hamptons. I decided to give up my apartment in Brooklyn and put all my stuff in storage. I had a bag with a toothbrush, clothes, and books always ready to travel. Life was certainly exciting, but beneath the movement and the fancy places, I couldn't shake that loneliness. I was thirty-six and wanted love. No amount of money in the world can make you feel like you're living a full life, if you just don't feel like you can be yourself. I realized I needed my people around me. I knew I was supposed to be doing more, learning more, challenging myself in different ways.

When I was back in NYC, Denise asked me to cook a celebratory family dinner the night before her daughter's bat mitzvah. And she asked me to make my curry chicken.

There were about thirty people for that dinner. I had asked my friend Nadine to help. We were co-workers at the Corner Bistro and we'd developed a deep connection quickly. I was happy she was there for support. I don't know if it was an especially amazing curry chicken I made. I wish I could remember *exactly* what I did or whether I had done anything different from the usual. Everyone loved the food. People came to the kitchen raving about the curry, asking for the secret ingredient.

Then Denise's brother, Ben, who was visiting from the UK, came in and started up a conversation. *Where are you from, what's your background, how long have you been cooking?* Small talk.

"Your food is incredible."

Maybe I was getting used to compliments, getting used to extravagant talk. I remember feeling flattered, but I didn't realize at first how serious he was.

"I want to help you out," he said.

"What do you mean?"

"I want you to be able to do what you do best. At the bat mitzvah tomorrow, I want you to tell me how much money you'd need to start your own business, or to do whatever you've dreamed of doing."

What?

I had heard about angel investors, and I'd been spending enough time with rich people to get kind of used to money meaning something different to them.

But I was fucking floored.

"Seriously?"

"Think about it. Think about a number and talk to me tomorrow."

I ran to Nadine and told her what had happened.

And, oh, I thought about it. I went from confused to elated to terrified for the rest of the night—no sleep—and into the next day.

Never mind how beyond my imagination it was to say that kind of thing to a stranger just because you liked her curry. My sleepless head focused on other questions. What was my worth? How could I possibly determine that? Was I a really good cook? I'd learned a lot since I stared helplessly at my mother's fridge. I'd made some families feel good and was totally confident in my abilities, but I wasn't a name, a star, some kind of quantifiable phenomenon with awards or even a restaurant as proof of my worth.

I was a bundle of nerves arriving at the bat mitzvah. Nadine was there as my guest and her presence calmed me. They had rented out a vast warehouse with access to the roof. After the ceremony, Ben said we should go up to the roof to talk. Standing above the noise and excitement of Manhattan, he asked me if I'd given his offer some thought. I said, "Yes, of course, and it's such a generous offer."

"How much would you need?"

I'm embarrassed when I think back at this, because honestly I would have felt grateful for a hundred bucks. Maybe I really had been spending too much time with rich people. When you hear the number, focus on the question mark, or ask yourself how much you would ask for.

"Five hundred thousand?"

He didn't bat an eye, or laugh.

"I'm not going to give you half a million, but I *will* give you a hundred thousand."

One hundred thousand dollars!

Forget that I had over-reached. That figure, one hundred thousand, was a fortune to me. I kept saying it over in my head. This man was giving me one hundred thousand dollars to make whatever dream I had come true. He said he'd have the money transferred into my account the following day. I floated downstairs, back into the bat mitzvah celebration, and embraced the moment.

Toasting to generosity. Toasting to the future. I'd won the lottery. I asked Ben's girlfriend why he'd want to give me money.

She didn't seem surprised. "He believes in people. He must believe in you."

And I believed in Nadine. For a while I thought we might be able to use the money to start a project together—a café or a catering company—but it turned out that we both had different visions, and besides, he had given the money to me. The possibilities were endless but I didn't want to feel rushed or pushed into anything. I needed to advocate for myself but I was torn and felt guilty, and it was a difficult decision for me to make. Ultimately, I had to do what was best for me. I decided to deposit the money and to wait for the right project to come along. It ended up breaking our friendship.

I remember calling my father the morning after the bat mitzvah to share the news.

"What did you do for him? What do you have to give him in return?"

That was his response.

He couldn't believe that someone would give me that much money simply because he liked my curry. He thought I must have offered something in return.

I couldn't believe how he saw me. That he would think that I'd sell myself for money, or that I'd say yes to a relationship where I'd owe this man forever.

He continued interrogating me, and I just tuned out. I knew the whole thing would seem crazy to him, and that at the centre of it all, he was just protecting me, but I was too excited to care.

"He thinks I'm a great cook, Daddy. That's all."

I was exactly where I was supposed to be, doing the thing I most loved that night. Cooking the food that teaches me about my culture, my people, my heritage, and my traditions. I suspected Denise played a part. But as I hung up with my father, a warming calm came over me. I felt my mum's presence. This was a blessing. An offering. A gift.

I sat on the money for almost two years, unsure of what to do. It was waiting for me when I returned from Paris, and it eventually became the seed money for my first restaurant, Saturday Dinette.

My days working as a private chef for Patty and Mark were often monotonous and lonely, but I wouldn't have changed them for the world. I learned a lot about myself during that time. I learned that without deep human connection I don't feel alive and fulfilled. I also discovered that I have a huge affection for France. I had fallen madly in love with Paris. Simple, but true. Having the chance to live in Paris was remarkable, and when Patty and Mark were ready to return to the States, I realized I didn't want to go back. I also realized that I didn't want to work for them anymore.

On one of my last days in Paris I met a friend for lunch. We were on the train heading to the restaurant, and someone overheard me mention to her that I wanted to learn more about French pastry. Pastry had always fascinated me and there was something other-worldly about the patisserie I ate in Paris. The baguettes. The croissants. Mmm. The warmth and butter consume you. It truly is an out of body experience. Un taquin, a tease. Many were delicate and light; some were elaborate and seemed to contain the entire history of French cuisine. The American woman who overheard me on the train suggested I look into Gastronomicom, a culinary school in Southern France. I really do believe in being in the right place at the right time. A random person, a complete stranger suggests something and I, of course, have to go deep and find out more. I did some research into the school, and it didn't seem like the tuition was too high, and it would extend my time in France. I decided to give them a call. I was immediately sold.

Quitting my job with Patty and Mark was a relief, but it wasn't easy. I don't think most people leave them, and even though I offered to train my replacement, Patty didn't take it well. She was annoyed and upset. I don't think it had anything to do with her feeling affection for me, it was quite simply that it was a change, and she'd have to get used to someone else in her life. Her reaction made it even clearer to me that I'd made the right decision. I flew with them back to Miami from Paris, and then I planned to return to France a few months later. In Miami, I borrowed my dad's car and cleared out my stuff from the apartment owned by Patty and Mark. They left for New York City without saying goodbye.

I spent my weeks in Miami with my family and friends, and during that time my best friend Amanda and I made plans to open a restaurant when I returned there from France. We were going to call it Roucou, after the red fruit that comes from the achiote tree, which is found throughout the Caribbean and South America. We even found a property that was perfectly unique, but a bit of a challenge: a three-bedroom family house within the commercial property line of the Design District in Miami that we would have to refit to become a restaurant. We wanted it to be homey and special. We wanted to build a show-stopping feature in the backyard—a fire pit—where we'd do some of the cooking. We could see it all, a busy, bustling restaurant that would be inspired by Caribbean cuisine and the limitless fresh ingredients available in Miami.

I daydreamed about the restaurant on my flight back to Europe (passing through London first to see my brother Wayne) and then on the train to the seaside resort of Cap d'Agde and final stop Gastronomicom. Cap d'Agde is right on the Mediterranean Sea, and it's surrounded by national parks. It's also well known for its nudist colony, but that's not where I was headed. I arrived in spring, so everything was alive. The train passed fields of yellow canola flowers, and deep-green hills, purple-blossomed trees, and quiet hamlets. Cap d'Agde is at the same latitude as Toulouse and just a little further south than Montpellier. As the train started to slow down, I saw that the town looked small and sleepy, and rain was about to roll in. Rain wasn't going to stop this fire.

Gastronomicom was founded by restaurateur Martine Lessault, who wanted to open a school where students from around the world could learn French culinary arts. Because Cap d'Agde is located in a pre-eminent wine region, they soon added a wine component as well as a French pastry course. Wines from the area—Languedoc, Roussillon, Fitou, etc.—are often earthy and rustic, with Syrah and other Rhone varietals predominating. Students could choose a one-month, three-month, or year-long program, and I had decided on staying just the month. Pastry and wine were compelling, but so was the idea of getting back to Miami to build the restaurant with Amanda.

I had signed up for a shared apartment, both to save money and to meet people, and when the bus from the train station dropped me at the school, I was given the key. The place was perfect. Three bedrooms, a kitchenette, and a sitting area, and a roommate who happened to be on the same train and bus as me. We hit it off right away, and our connection only deepened as we negotiated the weeks at school and the weekends travelling around the area.

I was thirty-seven years old, and I felt more free than I had in a long time. I felt open to adventure and the possibility of love in a way I hadn't really had time to experience in years.

The first time I saw him, he was wearing a white T-shirt and leaning against a wall. His shirt was wet as the rain had been steady all afternoon. He looked at me, and I looked back, and I saw his blue eyes, and his shaggy salt-and-pepper beard. He had a bald head, a warm face, and a presence about him that seemed approachable and safe. We held each other's gaze, and I smiled when I looked down; we'd both been caught.

A little later, five minutes to be exact, I walked out of the main office into the convenience store within the complex of our residences, and I thought of him again. He wasn't standing against that wall, though, and I filled my head with groceries instead: tea (my mum speaking to me again), bread, cheese, wine, maybe some sliced meat. I was in France, and I was going to eat like the French!

As I turned down an aisle, it was him again. The white T-shirt guy, basket in hand. We were both a little shy, but there was definitely some electricity. I waited for him to say something, I wanted to know how heavy his French accent was, and whether he spoke English. My French was terrible. I could order breakfast at a restaurant or ask for mushrooms at the grocery store. Living in Paris gave me the confidence to point and spit out the French word, but I had almost no conversational French at all.

I was here to learn about French pastry and wine. Focus, girl. Focus.

On my way back to my apartment, there was a gathering of people outside one of the other buildings. Someone yelled, "Hey, are you that New Yorker?" I turned and nodded. They invited me to join them for a glass of wine. It seemed pretty harmless, and I thought it would be good to meet some other students, especially when we shared the same language. I learned that one of the girls was from Georgia and another from Canada. They were all from the wine program, and they'd already spent three months at Gastronomicom; a family. The woman from Georgia explained that the apartment belonged to their classmates, Johnnie and Son. As she said their names, out walked my white T-shirt guy. An Australian of Greek heritage. Johnnie Karas.

Johnnie was at the very end of his Gastronomicom experience, and from the moment of that introduction, we realized that we had four days together before he left for a job at a restaurant in Mougins, a small town further north. I went to a party at their place the next night where we talked for hours, and we went to a cold and windy beach the day after, where we walked and talked more. I was stunned by how comfortable I felt with him. I wondered if it was simply the romance of the place, but it felt like something deeper. I decided to find out.

Classes started the next morning. The first half of the day was all about pastry, and the second half focused on wine. While my initial

desire to attend the program was centred on learning about French pastry-making techniques, I actually learned much more about wine. I had known almost nothing about it. The first blind tasting I did in Cap d'Agde was a choice between three wines that the instructor poured. He asked us to identify them and my response was: red wine?! I had a lot to learn.

The school was a mid-eighties European warehouse, with a single-level kitchen, industrial gas ovens, and stainless-steel countertops. White and pristine. They had interesting state-of-the-art quick-freeze tabletops for making ice cream or other chilled dishes, and there was a full sous-vide station at one end of the room. The modern electric deck ovens had the capacity to steam and proof, things that are central to making French pastries and breads.

I didn't know European measurements and temperatures, which immediately put me behind. There was only one pastry instructor, Pierre, for each class, and I quickly learned that wasn't enough. Pierre and I didn't get along from the get-go. He was arrogant and unapproachable and had no time for beginners. I'd been blessed with my experiences at the Natural Gourmet Institute and at my *stage* placements in Hawaii—I hadn't had to deal with the stereotypical know-it-all chef. I guess there's a first for everything. I was old enough and had spent enough time in New York City not to allow myself to get pushed around, and I wasn't going to start here. It was a bad beginning, but not for lack of will.

Of all the recipes we learned, I felt most connected to the creation of baguette. It's tricky bread to make because of the high hydration in the dough, and the wet dough is challenging to handle. Regardless of that, though, I eventually came to love the folding of the dough, the shaping and resting, the understanding that the yeast was living and dancing and making it possible for the bread to rise. It felt ancient and also totally in the moment.

I walked away from the pastry course with over one hundred recipes, but because of the breadth and complexity of French baked goods, I learned a little bit about each category of pastry, rather than a lot about a few. A little bread making, some chocolate making, very little about macarons. The art of petit choux, the proper way to fold a mixture—I learned about butter!—but everything felt a bit rushed. They were trying to do too much. There are certainly a few of the recipes that I go back to often, and that have made appearances on a collection of my menus. The pâte à choux recipe I learned and a classic French chocolate cake I also make frequently.

On Wednesdays we took trips to local wineries, which was where the real learning happened for me. The concept of terroir has shaped everything I've done since. I had an introduction to terroir in Hawaii, and learned from the farmer we visited about how the soil, climate, and his farming practices affected the taste of his vegetables. The flavours were specific to that plot of land.

On our journeys to wineries in the area surrounding Cap d'Agde I learned that the environment is heavily influenced by the Pyrenees Mountains, and the breezy coastal climate makes for salty, dry soil and air. These environmental factors shape how the grapes grow and how the wines taste and smell.

I learned how to identify specific flavours, to talk about maturity and freshness. The vocabulary was completely new to me. I might have used similar words to describe a painting or a photo, or a dish—bright, bold, challenging—but I was learning how to use them to describe flavours as well.

On one excursion we drove to Domaine du Météore in the village of Cabrerolles in the foothills of the Haut-Languedoc mountains. Grapes for the wines made by this winery grow in and around a crater made by a meteor that crashed to earth ten thousand years ago.

An old dog lifted his head in greeting when we piled out of the vehicle, and wind chimes sounded above him. The place had a hippie vibe. The winemaker took us on a tour of the vines and the processing room, and told us the story of how they harvest the grapes on the full moon. Their connection to the earth and the solar system gave me goosebumps. We were a talkative group, but in that space we were quiet—each of us taking in the moment. We drove a circular path over broken rocks and limestone toward the bottom of the crater. The way the van rocked back and forth, it felt like the Mad Tea Party ride at Disney World.

Creative people inspire me. The wine these *vignerons* were creating was incredible. It had hints of minerality and floral notes, and I could taste this specific place in the glass. The water that nourished the vines and the soil from which they grew were right there in the liquid I was swishing around in my glass.

The van got stuck in a rut as we tried to drive out of the crater that day. One by one we got out and tried to push the van as the driver floored the pedal. It just went deeper and deeper into the hole. Jerome, our instructor, decided to walk back up to the winery to get help.

"Guys, we're stuck in a crater and the sun is setting, who can say this isn't going to be the best story of our lives?" someone said. We all laughed. "Anyone thirsty?" Hands flew up. A bottle opener was passed around and we opened a few bottles of wine that we'd purchased. Drinking it, I could see the grapes that it was made from. The sound of crickets mixed with our laughter as the sun went down. We were all speechless.

There's only so much you can learn in a classroom, and theory can only take you so far. I need to experience things for them to sink deep. Settle in. That was also the case with the weekend trips I did with my roommates. We travelled to towns around Cap d'Agde to try different restaurants and bars, and one weekend we drove southwest for six hours to San Sebastián, Spain.

I was overwhelmed. Elated. Cobblestones and narrow streets, a kind of history my North American eyes hadn't seen. It made me realize that I didn't need more training, I needed to live. Watching how the restaurateurs interacted with the guests, the ease with which they brought out dish after dish of simple yet beautifully presented food. I remember a grilled octopus dish that was so simple—just octopus cooked on a grill, drizzled with olive oil and a pinch of salt. But the way those flavours and textures worked together—the creaminess of the octopus, the floral nature of the local olive oil, and the smokiness of the grill. Again, like the wine, I was understanding terroir: a story in my mouth about a very specific place.

The menus that I've created don't rely on food trends; they rely on finding the best ingredients and letting them shine. I want guests to remember the taste of the sea, the salt, the air. The textures that massage your tongue, and the desire to eat more and more. Just like I remember from San Sebastián.

We ended the night at a dive bar full of bikers, and as the only Black woman, I got some attention. An hour in and everyone was calling me "New York," and my roommates and I were sitting on the backs of Harleys in the parking lot. We moved on to hard liquor, which made for a long, painful night back at the hostel. I was sicker than a dog.

Hangovers and lovesickness sometimes work hand in hand. The first two weeks away from Johnnie, we spoke every day on my local phone and over Skype. He called between lunch service and dinner service at the restaurant, and these calls were our opportunity to get to know each other. Learn about our families, our travels, our dreams, and to think about the future. A little phone sex. My comfort with him continued to grow and I opened myself up to him. I told him about my plan to open a restaurant with Amanda, but I was starting to imagine him in that picture, too. With just under two weeks left at Gastronomicom, I knew I didn't want to leave France just yet. Johnnie and I decided that he would quit his job in Mougins, and we'd spend a month together in Nice.

I had some doubts. What if we didn't get along? What if he was really just a creep? What if I get trapped? And as usual, I ignored my fears and stepped forward.

We hadn't seen each other for a month, but when we met at the train station, it all came back. The nervous joy when I saw his blue eyes. Our first night, we stayed in Cannes at a small hotel. We were young school kids wanting to explore each other's bodies. I would fall asleep in the "nook" nestled in his arms, drooling on his chest. In the morning we would take a bus to Nice, Johnnie holding my hand as we walked to the apartment he had found for us. A busy Saturday, and the city felt alive. The main street, the Promenade des Anglais, was packed with people, and all along the water, vendors had set up umbrellas for rental. The beach was rocky, so people sat on chaises longues rather than right on the ground.

We didn't want to spend too much money; Johnnie needed to find a job, and I had already used some of the 100K to pay for my time at Gastronomicom. I wanted to save the rest. But we both had our own little savings, so we rented a small place in the old town that we could afford. Old Nice is so special and maze-like. Stores selling trinkets and groceries, dozens of cafés where people sat outside enjoying the day. There was an Irish pub at the end of our street, and that's how Johnnie knew where to turn. We arrived at an old wooden door, which he unlocked, then up two flights of stairs to apartment 2. It was tiny but sweet, with a balcony overlooking the cobblestone street, and right underneath us was a halal roasted chicken stand. Intoxicating aromas. Windows in the bedroom had accordion-style blinds, and there was a museum right across the street that explored the architecture of Nice.

It was full-on spring in Southern France, and Johnnie found a job on a luxury yacht in Antibes. I wandered through the streets and down to the beach and felt perfectly free. On one of his days off, we had just made love, a breezy day blowing our chiffon curtains. I was asking myself: What do I want from this? I have to go back to my life in the States. I felt such a connection to Johnnie. I realized it that day. I didn't feel inferior, or that I wasn't pretty enough, or smart enough, sentiments that once haunted me while dating Marty. Those feelings had been dispelled somewhat by a few other short-term partners, but they can be hard to shake completely. With Johnnie, I felt sexy, independent, smart, and dynamic. Maybe this was the person I could do things with—run a business, have a family. I was thirty-seven; he was thirty-nine. These were things we were both thinking about. Lying in bed, he put one arm around me, and I put my head on his chest. He'd say "get in the nook," and I would feel safe. I knew that I loved him.

I surrender to whatever love is.

Come in and stay.

We walked around the city a lot, both with this deep desire to learn and understand the culture. On one of our walks, we saw people standing in line and thought they were waiting for pizza. They were actually gathering around a huge paella pan and a man pouring what looked like pancake batter into it. Beside him was a sign that read "socca." We joined the line, and socca became one of my all-time favourite dishes. A crispy, creamy crêpe-like dish made from chickpea flour, water, and olive oil, and served with more olive oil on top and a sprinkle of salt. It's rolled up and served on a paper plate, and it's the perfect protein punch. At the Natural Gourmet Institute, we did a course on Italian food, and one of the recipes we made was panelle (Sicilian chickpea fritters). I learned that socca probably originated in Italy and was brought to Nice in the nineteenth century by Genoese immigrants. Nice at that time was a village where people lived mostly on fishing, olive oil, and tobacco, and socca was eaten at snack time by fishermen, dock-workers, and small traders. It's usually served with a glass of rosé, which makes it even more delicious!

Eating socca had me on tilt, and I knew I wanted to create a dish that was simple, street food, comfort food. It would eventually become an important dish for me—chickpea flour, ricotta cheese with lavender (that was the French connection), and confectioner's sugar. It was the perfect dish, one that went back to our days in Nice when Johnnie and I were first getting to know each other and falling in love. It was one of our favourites, and it became very popular with our guests.

We both cooked, and it was the first time I'd been with someone who was as interested in food as I was. We had a small two-burner stove and a tiny, under-the-counter fridge, and we shopped almost every day. Six eggs, baguette, cheese, wine—the stereotypical French experience. We made coq au vin using the halal chicken from downstairs. Salads of plump tomatoes with perfectly salted mozzarella. Grilled cheese with caramelized onions on local baguette. Peeled asparagus tips with olive oil.

Johnnie had the opportunity to apply for a job as a seasonal chef for a high-end camp north of Nice, where guests would come to stay in log cabins and experience the great outdoors. It was in parkland northwest of Nice, and we drove through Grasse and the perfumery region of France to get there.

We arrived in a sleepy resort with a creek running through it and a little house, where Johnnie had an interview. He was a confident man. I knew he could work hard. He didn't end up getting the job, but I started daydreaming about possibilities again. As I sat in the car waiting for him, I imagined us taking over the kitchen there, swimming, cooking, making campfires, and experiencing life in France. My nerves started to kick in, and a stream of questions filled my mind. How were we going to do this? Should I move here for good? Should Johnnie come to the States? We didn't want the story to end.

I knew I wanted to be a business owner. I wanted Johnnie to share that excitement. He wouldn't immediately be able to come to the States because he didn't have a visa, but a girl could dream, right? We both wanted to find a way to make it work, and in the morning he took me to the train station so I could catch a flight out of Paris back to Miami, I told him that I loved him and that I'd see him on the other side. I was wearing a blue striped shirt and military-green pants, and while he held my hands and kissed me goodbye, he told me we'd figure it out.

FOUR

# SATURDAY DINETTE

*Tiddeh fi mi tomorra fi yuh*

When I think of Saturday Dinette, I think of the purest joy and the deepest pain. My first restaurant. The kitchen that saw me through pregnancy, and my son's first two years. The counter where Johnnie and I sat and argued about menus and bigger, more complicated things. The place our love was challenged and solidified.

We made the restaurant into something special. It had big windows, clean lines, white tiled floors with black grout, and a long counter with retro leather stools. Yellow and olive-green wallpaper like you'd see in a sixties living room. Hand-painted silhouettes of seventies pin-ups. We always had records spinning: Prince, Stevie Wonder, John Coltrane, Tina Turner, Run-DMC, Roberta Flack.

We moved to Toronto's East End neighbourhood of Riverdale because it was affordable. My brother and my cousins, aunties, and uncles lived in the West End, Scarborough East, and Markham. Family surrounded me from all sides; I was truly supported. At the time, the East End was a little more rundown, there weren't very many restaurants, and the night life was almost non-existent. Johnnie and I found a loft—a live/work space that suited our needs and that's where Pepper and Sprout Catering was based.

The East End reminded me a little of Bushwick, Brooklyn, before the hipsters arrived: desolate, yet you could sense that something was coming. Riverdale is right in between two of my favourite neighbourhoods—Little India and Toronto's East Chinatown. That closeness to those two places and their incredible restaurants and shops made me happy. Made me miss Brooklyn. I could walk to Lahore Tikka for fish curry, or to Pearl Court for Chinese food and dim sum. I immediately felt at home in Riverdale.

We were never looking for a restaurant space. We had dreams of having pop-up dinners in our loft and really rocking the catering thing. Our loft was unique. We'd converted a 1200-square-foot raw space with a fifteen-foot ceiling and a large window at the back that we covered with baby-blue crushed velvet curtains. We had a test kitchen, an open-concept office space reminiscent of a Manhattan loft, and a bed frame and dresser Johnnie designed from wooden pallets. This was our haven, Johnnie's doing. He was fascinated by affordable structural material for a more modern, DIY home renovation. In the loft we had the flexibility and the square footage to turn that space into whatever we wanted.

Then we saw a small corner spot at Gerrard Street and Logan Avenue.

Plans changed.

As we drove by one day, we both commented on how cute the place was. It was called Mary Smith. We saw through the windows that the owners had a vintage retro decor, an homage to classic North American diners. It had that timeless vibe.

Logan Avenue was a neighbourhood street running right through Leslieville intersecting at Lake Shore Boulevard due south and into the Danforth neighbourhood to the north. The only businesses near that corner were an auto mechanic specializing in German cars, a plaza with a beer store, and a family-run coffee shop called Dog House Café. It really was a residential neighbourhood—some houses screaming generational wealth, others that were smaller and looked more like rental places. There wouldn't be a lot of foot traffic, but there was a streetcar stop right in front of the restaurant, which was at least something.

We made that corner of Gerrard and Logan part of our everyday driving route, and each time we drove by, the restaurant was closed. Every time. Then one day we saw a sign in the window: FOR LEASE.

I told Johnnie to stop the car. I called the number.

We went inside the next day and loved it—it had ready-made character and more possibilities with renovations. "Great bones," Johnnie said. He grew up in restaurants most of his life, working, building, and inspecting. His father owned a respected and famous no-menu restaurant called Jimmy's in Melbourne, Australia, for over twenty years. Johnnie knew what to look for.

The owners told us a bunch of people were interested (probably bullshit), and we went home immediately and drew up a business plan. And a few days later, it was ours.

Standing with Johnnie in the restaurant after we signed the contract.

"Is this for real?"

⁂

"Passports, please."

It's just over a year before Johnnie and I sign the contract, and we're at the Canada–US border crossing near Buffalo, New York. We've spent a few days in Toronto with my Canadian family, and we're heading home to Florida. We're going to stop in New York City to go to a Halloween party with my NYC friends and my sister, and to spend a couple of days in the Big Apple. I'm excited and happy, and I have some big news to share with them.

We're getting married.

A few days before, at the Archive Bar in Toronto, Johnnie proposed. I knew something was up because he seemed particularly nervous, and then a flood of feelings came out: how he felt about me, how much joy was in his life, and how excited he was to start a life with me in Miami. He had a little box in his hand, and in it was a coin that his mother had given him, passed down from his great-great-grandfather. He was planning to make it into a ring for me.

We've known each other for only a few months, but they've been intense. We were together every single moment in Nice, and he had flown to Florida to see me. They were months packed with travel, promises, and possibility.

We have rented a great apartment in Miami and have launched Pepper and Sprout Catering, which is already taking off. My dream to open Roucou with Amanda has faded a little in France. I love her like a sister, but I've fallen in love with a new dream, and with the possibility of working with Johnnie.

With Pepper and Sprout, he and I cook for film and television crews, Miami expats, fashion studios, photo teams—anyone I connected with when I freelanced for production companies in Miami. We cook on-site, beside a bright-green truck that we called Elle, making chilled cauliflower soup, whole roasted chickens, charred *haricots verts*—all of our French inspiration has survived the journey to Miami. Everything is on vintage platters and big, family-style plates. We stand out. People love our attention to detail and our food.

The future looks as bright as that sun.

We hand over our documents, and the border guard shakes his head. Johnnie's European visa was expired, not allowing him to re-enter the States. We're given two options: we can stay in Canada, or I can drive him to an airport immediately. I'm confused and pissed, and I have no idea what to do.

I turn the truck around and drive back to my half-brother Headley's place in Toronto. Johnnie can't afford to fly back to France to renew his visa, and we're not sure he'll be able to get one immediately anyway.

Looks like we're staying in Toronto.

Our decision to move to Canada was made for us. Pepper and Sprout changed from a Miami-based entity to a Toronto-based one.

Sitting on the bed in Headley's guest room, I asked myself some hard questions. Did I want to move to Canada so I could be with a man I'd met only months before? Did I want to be a wife? Was this the right time? And what about all my friends and family in Florida? How could I live without them? I was confused. Heartbroken. And even though Johnnie was with me, I felt strangely alone.

After a few days of misery, I got up and decided to throw myself wholly into making Toronto work. I thought about my mother and how she hadn't been given a choice to move to the UK. Or, later, to the US. And I thought about her landing in Canada to escape her abuser. I was lucky. I was in love, and I was in a country that made me feel connected to her. I had uncles and aunties, cousins and a fiancé. I could totally make this work.

And remember that 100K? Well, that allowed us to open the Dinette.

Remove the drop ceiling. Drywall. Turn the music up. Lay the tile. Resurrect the art of wallpapering. Breathe in gypsum, sawdust. Make love.

Work all day and all night. Light a spliff.

We were trying to save money, and I guess in theory it made it feel more "ours," but doing the renovations ourselves was a crazy amount of work. And during that time, we planned our wedding. January 25, 2014. We had it in our loft. Take the mattress off the pallets and turn it into an altar.

I'll walk down the aisle in our makeshift chapel to the song "Prototype."

Charmaine, my cousin, will lead us in prayer, then declare *You're man and wife.*

We'll dance.

We'll ignore the skeptical looks from our guests.

*They hardly know each other.*

We'll eat Black Cake. Made in a jar under the counter.

Black plums. Dried cherries. Raisins. Cinnamon. Vanilla. Overproof white rum.

*Leave the fruit, drunk, submerged in the sugar.*
*Sugarcane.*
*Black skin.*
*An offering to guests.*
*Placed in a box, sealed with the love that we're celebrating.*
*Marriage.*
*Crumbs under the nails.*

During the renovations, I'd look over at Johnnie and think, *Okay, I made the right decision.* He's such a hard-working guy, and he made the heaviest days feel lighter. He's funny and he makes me feel good about myself. There was so much we didn't know about each other, but it didn't matter at that point. I forgot that I'm a sun-lover, not a skier.

We opened in 2014, and that first autumn was challenging. Initially, I envisioned the Dinette as the kind of diner you'd find in Brooklyn. I was missing the familiarity of New York, and I wanted to bring some of that vibe to Riverdale. Cool, relaxed atmosphere. Super tasty food. Affordable. We initially served classic Jewish diner fare: matzo ball soup (although we made it into a gumbo), latkes (we made them with sweet potatoes or zucchini instead of yellow potatoes), homemade gravlax with beet sugar (absolutely delicious, but hardly anyone ordered it). I'd perfected a number of Jewish dishes while working for Martina (my Russian family), Denise, and Marissa, and before that, I'd fallen in love with Jewish cuisine while in middle school and high school. Blintzes stuffed with potato or jelly, latkes with apple sauce and sour cream, chocolate rugelach, and crispy kugel. It was comforting to me, and that's what I wanted the restaurant to do: to comfort with honest, delicious food.

Before we took over the space, in one of its many incarnations, it had been a Greek restaurant. It was run by a man named Jimmy, and for the first few months, people would still come in looking for his inexpensive breakfast plates. We'd say, *There's no Jimmy, but we've got a Greek Johnnie, and why don't you try our food?* Sometimes they did, but more often than not, they'd leave. We were trying to figure out what people wanted, how much they wanted to spend, and, ultimately, how to become a part of the neighbourhood.

We played around with the menu. We replaced things and tried other classics (baked chicken thighs, hot buttered crusted pies with mushy peas, sticky braised beef back ribs, and a classic 80/20 burger).

By November we were starting to get a little busier, but something wasn't quite right. That's when I started digging deeper. Somehow the food I was making didn't feel like it was authentically mine. It was an unexpected feeling. As a private chef, I was proud of my ability to cook anything the client wanted. And I loved the French countryside–inspired dishes I was making for Pepper and Sprout, right before we opened the Dinette. Every dish I made, I made with love, and people enjoyed what I cooked.

The Dinette felt different, though. I guess I was putting more pressure on myself. We were a brick-and-mortar establishment, and because of that, I wanted it to be a clearer representation of myself. Welcome to *our* space, this is *my* food. Johnnie encouraged me to rethink the menu, again, and as I was standing at the counter, looking at our wall of photos, it came to me.

There was a bright-red wall in the Dinette, right across from the kitchen pass, and on it was a series of framed black-and-white photos. One was Muhammad Ali after he won the 1964 fight in Miami against Sonny Liston. The fight that would change the world. It was the time of the civil rights movement, and Black people were fighting for their dignity and for their rights as human beings. There were a couple of photos of restaurants in the Southern US, and one of Martin Luther King Jr. staring out from a mug shot, the numbers 7089 around his neck. There were shots of lunch counters in the sixties in the South—a lone Black man refusing to leave the counter at Woolworth's in Greensboro, North Carolina, and a Black woman sitting next to a white woman at another restaurant.

Those photos meant everything to me.

It's 6 a.m., and Gerrard Street is still quiet. I've come in to prepare brunch. The sun is rising, and the light is yellow-pink and so delicately beautiful that I've dropped my bags on the floor and I'm standing in the middle of the restaurant. I can see my reflection in the window, and it's like I've become a framed picture on the wall of photos. Here I am, a Black, woman restaurant owner. I'm married to a white man, an incredible man.

I owe everything to those fierce activists: my mother, mother's mother, my ancestors. The Civil Rights movement. The battles fought in the foothills of Saint Elizabeth, Jamaica. The Million Woman March. Without them, I wouldn't be standing in my kitchen, trying to create a new menu in my restaurant.

When customers were seated at the table right underneath the photos, I would always glance over to see how they responded. Most would be smiling, *Okay, we're set, we actually got a table, let's eat.* They'd take off their coats, sit down, and then look up. And if they took notice, if they really looked, the smiles would fade, and they'd have a look of sadness. Sorrow. Empathy. The images reminding us of what came before.

In the sixties, Black students started protesting Jim Crow laws by peacefully sitting at lunch counters deemed "Whites Only." Quietly, they would sit and order, and when they were refused service, they would refuse to leave. They sat. They sat at counters that fed white people and treated Black people as if they were invisible. As if they didn't matter.

I loved the fact that we had an open kitchen in the Dinette. Our customers could see me and the other Black women who were cooking with me. We were centre stage. We were the stars. It made me happy to think back to the divide between front of house and back of house at Beard House with all my Black and Brown friends in the back and my invisibility as a private chef.

See me now.

So I started thinking about my years in the American South, as well as my connection to Canada. Florida, Atlanta, Toronto. Toronto is the place where my parents met, and where a big part of my family migrated to in the sixties. I started thinking about the movement (both forced and not) of Black bodies across oceans, and my own family's experience of being a part of the African Diaspora.

I realized that *my* story had to be on the plate. What was my food?

The first dish I made at the Dinette that felt like an authentic version of myself was our Big Chick Thighs. I resisted making it for a while—as a Black, female chef I didn't want to play into the stereotype of Black people only making fried chicken. It's such a controversial dish, a dish that comes with a racist past, and one that I found hard to accept.

When I first created the recipe for the Dinette's version, though, I felt joy. I was celebrating the history of Black food. Not just the pain of my past, but the strength of all Black women who used to sell fried chicken at train stations and on the street. Fried chicken gave a freedom to Black women who launched their entrepreneurial quest, unlocking them to flourish and establish their own independent economic strategies. Their ability as Black women to create something delicious with inexpensive ingredients made it a celebrated African American staple for special occasions. It morphed into a dish that felt like a nod to the resilience of Black women everywhere. But this was my version, and it would be baked, not fried.

Because of my training at the Natural Gourmet Institute, I played around with the recipe. As a health-supportive chef, I coated the chicken in chickpea flour, added fresh thyme and lemon zest, and then topped it with fried chickpeas.

The first time it appeared on the menu was as an appetizer, and I called it Big Chick Thighs, in honour of my sister. What we'd call each other was "Big Girl." My sister and I had struggled with our weight growing up in Plantation. Growing up in a Jamaican house. "You so fat," my grandmother would say, as she would slap my thighs. We were too fat for ballet or basketball, and my father was vocal to my mother about it. He would say, "Stop buying chips and junk, they don't need it." But she wouldn't listen. In response she would take us shopping at Burdines every Saturday. Pulling and tugging at the buttons. Slouched in the chair frustrated and daydreaming about being skinny. One day. We used food to make us smile. To heal us, to swallow pain and sadness. We started Big Girl out of wanting to find joy in ourselves and in our bodies. It made us laugh. It still does. That name was our celebration of us. Loving us together. It made me happy to call the dish Big Chick Thighs, and it became so popular we made it into a plate almost immediately. People would call ahead to reserve their plate.

Other dishes came afterward—braised pork chops with roasted apples, pan-seared chicken livers, and onions served with toast.

And grits. Oh, those damn grits.

My parents didn't cook grits; we ate wheat porridge and cornmeal porridge, a hot, comforting cereal. Grits are made of coarsely ground corn, and the first time I tried them was when I lived in Atlanta, served with salt and butter and biscuits. I can't say I was an immediate convert after that first experience, but I have deep appreciation for the history of grits, and I wanted to create my own take on the classic Southern dish.

I did tons of research and found that grits are based on a Native American dish that uses corn ground in a stone mill. The word "grits" comes from "grist," which is the name Indigenous people in Virginia gave to the dish.

As well, corn and corn scraps (and other cheap grains) made up a big part of the diet of slaves working on Southern plantations. Shrimp and grits can be traced back to the Gullah and Geechee peoples, descendants of slaves from West Africa who were forced to work and live in the South.

I wanted my grits to celebrate Indigenous and African American cultures. Cultures that took pride in transforming scraps into beautiful food—cornmeal grist, kush, porridge.

Customers wrote to me about the grits we served at the Dinette. They said things like *You completely changed the way I think about grits.* I loved making them. It felt ceremonial. Like I was connecting to the past, and to labour performed by my ancestors.

I started with locally sourced coarse-ground grits from K2 Milling in Ontario. I cleaned the dust off the husks, and then I steamed them. You don't want to rush the making of grits. In a wide-bottomed pot, on an even temperature, I cooked them until they had softened and fluffed up. Then I added the love. Salted butter. A local cheddar cheese that we shredded. A little whole milk. And the secret ingredient—a squeeze of lemon juice at the very end. That unexpected acidity is a chef's back-pocket secret. With fatty foods, if you add acidity, you create balance.

The lemon also has a natural sweetness to it, and the flavours played off one another perfectly.

Back in Brooklyn, after Kauai, I started something called the Green Table Project. I'd gone through Landmark Education (a personal-development program recommended by a friend), and the final piece of my learning was the Self-Expression Leadership Program. I had to design a project that empowered others and myself. I was totally inspired by Hawaii and healthy, sustainable food, and I decided to set up some cooking workshops at the YMCA in my neighbourhood. I used ingredients from community gardens in and around Brooklyn. We aligned with a neighbourhood community-supported agriculture program that donated any surplus vegetables to the project. Most of the participants were women from the community, aunties, and cousins, and we cooked together. We talked about nutrition, Black people, food justice, the challenges of sourcing good food, and accessibility in Black neighbourhoods. We shared recipes. It was amazing. It was my first real experience with food advocacy, and it has shaped everything I've done since.

In Toronto, looking to find a way to make the Dinette an active part of the community, I thought about the YMCA. Researching options, I learned that the YWCA offered mentorships and training programs for women and girls. They promoted equality, economic security, and violence-free futures. I knew there was something there.

"Johnnie, what if we create an all-female brigade? Open the Dinette with a kitchen full of female chefs?"

The Dinette's program became a co-operative training program that enlisted young women from several organizations like the YWCA. We would train the women in both front-of-house and back-of-house roles, menu planning, and business practices while they worked at Saturday Dinette. We were hoping to train the next generation of women in the culinary industry. Years later, in 2018, I was asked to present the project at a symposium in NYC called Women in Hospitality United.

I was making a social impact, teaching young women and increasing their confidence. But I learned a lot from them, too. One of the three young women, Heather, stayed with us for two years. She was a young mom from Scarborough, a quiet young woman full of potential but scared that we wouldn't see it. She was a blank canvas, but in the two years she was with us, she was able to run prep and jump on the line when we needed her. She was my right arm in those early months. Heather went on to take a number of pastry classes at George Brown College and eventually landed a role as kitchen manager at a good place close to home. She worked hard. She asked questions. I think there was a different light in her when she left us.

Sometimes in the hospitality industry, we have a "warm bodies" attitude, and staff are valued less than the ingredients. If someone can come to work and do the job relatively well, that's good enough. Instead, we wanted to empower them to be passionate in anything they do, encourage them to tap into their own strengths and trust the process and the work.

Respect for employees means that we tried to pay them well. Traditionally there's a separation between front of house and back of house, where those in the front kept the tips, while those in the back were paid a higher wage. Trying to balance the two never really worked, though, and we wanted everything to be shared equally.

We wanted to pay livable wages and make everyone behind the scenes—the people who are equally responsible for a restaurant's success—more visible.

It's the beginning of March 2015. Toronto is still squarely in winter, and it's frigid and dark, but there's a warm glow coming from the windows of the Dinette. The restaurant is packed. We have seats for twenty-three, but we've brought extra chairs from the basement. One group of four guests is crammed at a table for two, and they're eating from their laps because there's not enough room for their plates on the table. Classic soul music spins on the turntable, and Johnnie pours cocktails for the guests at the counter. He makes a fierce Dark and Stormy with spicy ginger, bitters, rum, lime juice, and ginger beer. The servers squeeze past tables, trying not to step on the sleeves of coats that have slipped from the backs of chairs. We have to crack the door because it's so hot.

Fat ankles.

I'm seven months pregnant.

On February 20, 2015, one of Canada's national newspapers, the *Globe and Mail* (I was still so new to Canada I didn't even know what that paper was), helped put us on the map. We had a photographer come a few days earlier taking pictures of me with the trout burger and sticky ribs.

The phone started ringing early, well before 2 p.m. "Sorry. we don't take reservations. We are a small restaurant," Johnnie said. He told me he was going across the street to grab a few copies of the paper. As he read it out loud, we all started getting excited. And nervous! As we were prepping for what should have been a normal busy Friday night, the phone kept ringing, and a few customers had come to the door asking if they could make reservations.

By then I had started really loving that little space. I certainly wanted the business to thrive, and we needed to make some money, but it also felt like we were inviting people into our living room. It had such a chill vibe that people would even bring their own records for us to spin on the turntable. Many of the guests became our friends.

I didn't know anything about the Toronto restaurant scene, and we weren't trying to be anything we weren't. The city seemed to be craving a new spot with an easygoing atmosphere. Our food was rich in history, honest, and delicious.

"Saturday Dinette: A Real Toronto Neighbourhood Finally Gets a Real Neighbourhood Diner," was the headline. The reviewer, Chris Nuttall-Smith, described our restaurant as "a corner diner like nobody's built them in 60 years," and went on in warm and surprised terms about the chicken, the lighting, the music. It was heart-warming to us, especially these lines about the staff: "The service, run both times I ate there by a preternaturally warm and competent 19-year-old, makes you wonder why so many more established, more expensive places can't get service this right."

Johnnie and I took it all in.

"Should I have ordered more chicken?"

My heart started racing, and I yelled to the team, "Okay guys, we are about to have the service we will never forget." I ran down to the staff area and grabbed my lip balm out of my bag, rushed to the washroom, and stared at my reflection. I shook my head and wiped away a few tears that got away, tucked my dreads into place and glossed my lips. *Breathe.*

"You got this."

Johnnie met me halfway up the stairs, and we kissed.

So nice.

Let me remember for a second.

You know, when I looked just now at that review again, after all the warm memories, there's a line that jumps out at me:

"Ms. Barr doesn't really know where home is, she says."

ATTENTION! ATTENTION! ATTENTION! BABY ARRIVING!

We made the announcement on our website and on a piece of paper on the front door of the restaurant. We let people know that I'd be taking a few weeks off. Then I'd return, and I'd be cooking with my baby on my back. It was a calm statement, a statement that exuded confidence—two things I was not feeling. I had no idea whether people would be patient enough to wait until we reopened, and I felt completely frazzled with the stresses of becoming a new mum combined with running a business that had just started to thrive. It was a challenging time. We even considered selling the business. We had an offer from a potential buyer, but our landlords got greedy and tried to screw things up. When we didn't accept the offer right away, the buyer lowered it substantially. We learned later that the landlords were trying to make a backdoor deal with the buyer. We called the offer bullshit, and after a pep talk with Johnnie's dad in Melbourne, Australia, we knew that we had to keep going. My mother's brother Raymond and his wife Veronica offered their support, and we forged ahead.

I'll think of Myles for a second, my little Myles.

Restaurant baby.

Hold him in one hand, spatchcocked and beautiful.

So, the *Globe* review has come out, the restaurant is finally on the map, we're busier than we ever have been, and I'm about to give birth. I think back to that day driving along the Gardiner Expressway when my doctor first told me I was pregnant. So much has happened in these few months, and although it's been a struggle, I'm excited about this baby growing inside me. I can't stop the thoughts that whirl around inside my brain, though: *We're finally doing good business, and we're going to have to close the doors for a while after I give birth. When we reopen, will the customers still be there?*

Being a pregnant chef is brutal. I'm on my feet sixteen hours a day, and my legs are impossibly sore. Morning sickness has forced me into the alley behind the restaurant many times to throw up, and on one occasion the fire department from just up the street was called because I passed out. Dehydration and exhaustion. I have to make a commitment to myself and to my growing belly that I will be more mindful, hydrate myself, and feed myself and not just my customers.

Working, working, and I'm sitting on the pregnancy stool Johnnie bought me (the only way he knew I would sit). I'm at the Dinette, rolling seafood balls. I honestly don't know what to expect from any of it, and that day I miss my mum in the deepest way possible. I am about to become a mother, and I mourn the fact that I can't share that with her. *How much is it going to hurt?* I keep thinking. *Can I do this?* I hope that maybe not everything I have heard about labour is true. "You will probably throw up." "You may shit yourself." "Oh and careful not to tear or rip."

*What the fuck?*

I think about my own birth and what Mummy must have felt and thought about. Was she scared? She had already done this twice before.

Will he look like Johnnie? Will he look like me? Blue eyes, brown eyes? Johnnie wants him to play soccer: it doesn't matter what he looks like, he just has to play for Liverpool.

What's it going to feel like to have a biracial child? Will people ask him, *Why don't your parents look the same?* He's going to be a Greek, Jamaican, Australian, Canadian Taurus.

Do I deserve to be a mother? Am I as good as my own? What do you do with a crying child? All those questions.

And we have no security. If the restaurant doesn't work, we have nothing. And how does the restaurant work when we have this child?

I really feel like we were giving birth to two things at once: the restaurant and our son.

I felt a hard pinch and a pain, and then a much deeper pain.

It was beginning.

My girlfriends Tahlia and Amanda had come from Florida for the birth, and I had my bag, a soundtrack, candles, incense. I was as ready as I could be.

I'm not going to say labour was easy.

It was mystical, visceral, moving, and impossible, and some of it I like to hold on to without words.

When his skin was on mine, he was all that mattered, and then that need, his needs, what Johnnie and I needed . . .

We were back at work after six weeks. The heat in the kitchen at any time of year was unbearable. My body had already been run-down before labour. Even though we weren't serving dinner, the workdays were still twelve hours long. Prepping, cleaning, ordering ingredients and supplies, managing staff. Myles was strapped to me a lot or he slept in his stroller behind the counter. I don't remember sleeping.

Johnnie was working his ass off and keeping so much of our life together. We didn't have time to talk.

I don't know how we did it.

But I have pictures in my head, some of them blurry, a lot of them warm. Our customers were such a help. By the time he was six months old, Myles was being passed around the restaurant like a basket of freshly baked bread, the shared love, and everyone wanting a sniff and a nibble.

Myles was slightly underweight, so we went from the midwifery clinic to the hospital when he was born. How many worries can you count as a parent? All the challenges you start imagining even before a child arrives.

Johnnie's mother asked shortly after he was born, "How dark is he?" I acknowledged that my father, too, would be curious. This baby would face racism different from my own. Was he Black, biracial? These labels and powerful stigmas.

Our role as parents will be to protect him. Guide him. Lead him. Learn from him. It had me reflecting back to my own issues with my own race. My younger self wanting to be someone else. Wanting to have long, silky hair.

A night nurse, a Caribbean woman, came into my room that first night in the hospital. She was beautiful. Sweet and friendly. Mothering and yet stern with her intentions. The doctor and nurses explained that if he was challenged latching on, he might have to go to the intensive care unit. She showed me how to position my nipple just above his tongue, not quite touching the roof of his mouth. I never got her name as I was fading in and out of sleep, mentally and physically exhausted from the twenty-six-hour birth experience.

Skin to skin, he lay on my chest.

Most of that worry you forget. This Myles I know now, he teaches us that love will surpass all cultural differences. This Myles that night so tiny, Johnnie asleep in a chair. It was our moment finally, me and my boy.

He watched me. His proud Black mother. I watched him slowly close his eyes. Open again.

We were latched.

We hit our stride by 2016, and that was my favourite year. We took on weekend brunch by then, and if I thought dinner was busy, brunch was hella crazy. Super long lineups, countless influencers with their phones and Instagram accounts that reached across the globe, and hours of insanity in the kitchen. With Myles strapped to my back in a sling, on some occasions he was the strength I needed. His dark brown eyes piercing my soul reminding me his love was unconditional, and Johnnie and I would never be alone. His little legs were chubby and full of folds, "He's a chunky one," folks said.

But as much as I always wanted him around, I needed help. My mother's brother Uncle Vernal and Aunt Sonia offered. I was still nursing when Myles started going to Auntie's house. Eventually my milk was not enough for him, so we gave him formula.

Amazing reviews of the Dinette kept coming, and as our notoriety grew, I started to become the face of the restaurant. There weren't many female-run kitchens in Toronto, and even fewer were run by Black women.

The recognition meant that I put even more pressure on myself. It also led to some tension between me and Johnnie because all of a sudden I was in the spotlight. It was our restaurant, but I was the face of the Dinette, and he started to resent that. But he would never admit it. A producer from the TV show *You Gotta Eat Here* came and shot an episode. Others came and so did more invitations. *Can we feature you on the show? Will you be a judge on the next season?* Days became even more packed, and I didn't really notice that Johnnie was more and more absent. We didn't always have time to sit down and catch up, and it turned out he was drinking way more than I knew.

Almost from the beginning we had tension with our landlords. They didn't want to hear our music, and they didn't want us in the building past 11 p.m. It was ridiculous. They lived right above the restaurant, but somehow they thought they wouldn't be able to hear anything. I'm still not sure why they rented the place to us, why they thought another restaurant was going to be the right tenant. It didn't take long for them to start pounding on our ceiling while we were in the middle of service. And then they started calling the cops with noise complaints. Never open a restaurant if the landlords live above you. Just don't do it.

It got bad. They threatened us all the time, one of them spat in Johnnie's face.

The stress was too much for both of us, and Johnnie coped by staying late at the restaurant and then going out. He would have some drinks to take the edge off, and then started getting into coke to keep himself alive for the next day's pressures. Of course I knew that he was stressed, but I didn't know till months later how he was coping. It almost broke us.

I'll tell you, I'll tell you.

Some of those memories, those evenings when we were closing, the light fading, the warmth of that place and the flavours in the air, the photos of my heroes. My dreams had come true, even dreams I didn't remember having. My little family, my restaurant. Strong, talented women in the kitchen with me: Tsion, Diane, Wolfgang, Kamoy, Ozioma. We had staff meals on Sundays, eating the leftovers and drinking half-emptied bottles of wine. Myles was almost two and dancing on the tiles, and everyone was comfortable. Those memories choke me up right now. Everyone went home with food, and Monday was our day of rest.

We renovated the Dinette and enlarged it to forty seats. We kept the soul music playing, and customers kept bringing in their own vinyl. I loved looking out from the kitchen and seeing familiar faces and new ones.

We focused on ways to avoid the complaints from our landlords.

About a year after we opened the Dinette, when we were still doing dinner, my dad came to visit. Daddy hates flying, so his visits from Florida are rare. But he wanted to visit the restaurant and see what all the fuss was about. I was more nervous for his visit than on opening night. I had a lot to prove. And aside from being a great cook, he was a great eater. Kind of a gourmet.

I still needed to show him that I'd made the right decision to leave MTV.

It was a Friday night, and the restaurant was bumping. Every table was occupied, and the room was loud with guests' voices and the four-on-the-floor beat of our house music mix. It was like my parents' house parties. My nerves. Man, I wanted him to be proud, to show him that we were a success. One of our staff members escorted him and his wife, Junie, to the counter where we'd reserved two stools. I wanted him to be next to the kitchen to see me cooking.

A Greyhound for my dad. Vodka, grapefruit juice, lime. White wine for Junie.

I made him sliced beef brisket with braised cabbage, carrots, and apple compote. Maybe I led the team with a little more self-consciousness, a little more control.

From the get-go he was impressed, surprised, totally taken by the food.

I kept glancing over to see his reaction, and he smiled. That light in his eyes. I'd done it. The room was bustling, customers were stopping by the pass to offer their gratitude, and he got a chance to witness it all.

His daughter followed in his footsteps and became a successful business owner.

And then, after almost three years, it was over.

I don't like even mentioning our landlords more than I have to, but they are the reason we closed. Noise complaints. Harassment. Constant, often strange interference, like reporting to the city that the range-hood wasn't to code—even though it was a lie. One busy brunch, the owner was standing outside the front window with a chisel, staring menacingly at the customers.

From the beginning, the restaurant was a refuge, a place of unimaginable peace. Even though we were working our tails off and never got a break, we had achieved so much, as a family and as a team. But the misunderstandings gathered, the complaints became constant. We were forced to do brunch instead of dinners because they didn't want the late-night noise. They called the cops when customers stood outside the door. They stomped on the floor above. Lawyers got involved.

When there's a bully upstairs, you change the way you walk, the way you behave, you become preoccupied and start tip-toeing instead of moving with joy, instead of turning up the music and dancing. Instead of embracing the change you were creating for the many lives and communities you were impacting.

You lose your dream, you get angry, you get sad.

You say fuck them.

I remember pushing a fridge across Gerrard Street. We'd been in the Dinette all weekend, taking out chairs, marble-top tables, the record player, albums—anger and a lump in our throats making everything heavier than it should have been. That fridge felt like I was pushing, shouldering, every disappointment and failure, every bad decision and mistake, everything in the world that was metal, grey, and cold.

Fuck them.

Three years after closing the Dinette, I still get messages from people saying how much they miss it.

# FIVE

# ENDURANCE

Pepper bun hot but it good fi curry

*S* *low* caramelization.

That's the key to a great French onion soup.

Johnnie knows. When we were in Mougins, France, we had onion soup that was unforgettable. When we tried to recreate it at the Dinette, that's what we learned to do—take time, let the process play out. And when I approach most of my dishes now, I would say that is my technique. I tell sous-chefs, "You have to let the food *cook*. Don't move it around all the time."

Maybe I should have followed my own advice when it came to living. Some of what happened next is a blur. Not feeling settled. Trying to find the next thing. Trying to get that feeling back from the Dinette. Wandering, trying, looking, definitely learning. Not quite finding my way home.

Johnnie and I brought all our tables and equipment a few doors further west to a space we found, a little smaller than the Dinette's. Kid Chocolate. We named the place after a Cuban boxer Johnnie was enamoured with. It was going to be Johnnie's project, his baby that I was obviously going to work hard at. Our plan was to make it into a late-night Afro-Caribbean cocktail bar with a steam table. Very cool, night-focused, no more brunch. We drew up menus and lined it all up, and then, of course, landlords. New ones. We had to secure building permits to do what we wanted to do. The permits took too long. There were pre-existing issues with the building. Kid Chocolate didn't step into the ring.

Calls and invitations came in. *Food & Drink* magazine, *Chatelaine*, the *Kit*, the *Toronto Star*, *BlogTO* they all wanted a piece of my story. What happened to Saturday Dinette? How did it fall apart when it was doing so well? Some of them I took, some I ignored. Too painful, too many memories. These were things that took me away from cooking, from creating. I was sensing a change in Johnnie and in our relationship, but I didn't know yet how badly he was struggling. I was just trying to keep it together as a parent. Is Myles safe, fed, loved?

Sadness. Frustration. Still some profound joy in being a parent.

We had no regular income, nothing to rely on, our equipment dragging behind us like the roots of a tree, pulled up and wind-tossed.

I can feel now how much I was trying to hit the ground running, to keep blinders on and not feel the grief of losing the Dinette.

Just before it closed, I was invited to create a menu at the Gladstone Hotel, to be a chef in residence, and I practically ran there. A historic hotel. Cool. Art-focused in Toronto's West End, the Gladstone had event spaces, rooms decorated by different artists, and a creative ambition that hung on every wall. It felt like a wonderful opportunity for me, if not a wonderful distraction. It turned out to be hugely important, but I need to skip over that for now. My habit of not sitting still, those blinders on my eyes . . . I was on a path to a pretty dark place. Me and Johnnie together.

He showed a lack of drive, which I hadn't seen before. He was struggling with so much. Everything was moving too slowly when it came to Kid Chocolate, and he was still exhausted from the Dinette. There was still some jealousy and restlessness. He was also scared.

While at the Dinette, he gave that place its heartbeat. He floated, eased through that room and behind the bar mixing up concoctions while charming with his accent. "You're from South Africa or England, right?" a constant question. Greek-Aussie boy. Difficult, wary guests—he made them relax. He remembered everyone's drinks and made suggestions for what they should have tonight.

He made small talk feel big, and people remembered him as much as he remembered them. "Remember to lick the plate . . . the chef appreciates the love."

His confidence was infectious and was a big part of why customers came back and felt comfortable.

If a table complained about the music being too loud, the server told Johnnie; he raised his head, looked back at the table, smiled impishly, and somehow his charm was so strong across the room that he could turn the music up a notch and the customers smiled and gave in.

I felt supported by him, completely secure when after a long day of prepping grits, cleaning mussels, folding biscuits, finishing sauces, and guiding my team, I had to take Myles home and leave the place in his hands. During those days, Johnnie built a beautiful bond with Myles. And he worked hard, staying at the restaurant late every night.

Last guest out, one more glass of wine.

Johnnie's dad was in the restaurant business, and Johnnie was a restaurant kid just like Myles—from the age of eight he was wearing a bow tie and working, getting old-school kicks in the ass from a hard-driving father. And sometimes he played as hard as he worked.

The hospitality industry can be a cruel space for anyone with a leaning toward addiction. The stress is so great, the hours so crazy, and with the availability of booze, good booze, and drugs, good drugs . . . the strongest people I know have succumbed. The desire for perfection that is rooted in the industry: you're never good enough, so try harder. The notion of breaking someone down to only bring them back up. That was not Saturday Dinette, but that was the world Johnnie had come from. That was his experience working in London in the late nineties, and in both Sydney and Melbourne (his hometown). And then as things fell apart, I knew why Johnnie leaned harder, I knew exactly why—I'd been walking every step with him. This grief I felt over losing our dream, that I wasn't really allowing myself to feel—he was feeling the same, and using a different set of tools to blind himself to it.

He grew remote, absent even when he was there. The Canada Revenue Agency was on our ass for a huge amount in back taxes, and vendors were calling in debts. Margins are tight in the restaurant business, and we had barely paid ourselves enough to live. I started blaming things on him, the responsibilities were *his*. *How could I take care of all this stuff* and *look after Myles?*

I was raised by a hard-working Black man who never showed vulnerability. No space for weakness. Onward and upward. No communication.

Needless to say, the space between us grew bigger.

Myles was three. People say the twos are the worst, the terrible twos, but in my experience, the threes make the twos look like a cute little puppet show.

I was exhausted, burnt-out, emptied.

Footprints in sand. That's what I wanted. The sun on my face. The sound of waves.

Watch Myles build sandcastles.

Sleep in the bed next to the window where that ackee tree still grows.

Run away.

Plantation. Go back to what I thought was home.

Myles and I got on a plane to Florida, leaving Johnnie behind, and flew to see my dad and old friends.

In Florida I rested. As much as you can with a three-year-old. I found a daycare close to my father's house. I dreamed about making a plan; something fresh, a new position, a new life, starting over once again. A quick gig cooking for a celebrity, exploring options.

I went to the beach with Myles; my father grew a relationship with his grandson. I went to Miami to see my friends and remember my life before. I talked on the phone to my sister, who lived in Los Angeles.

She told me I'd be a fool to go back to Johnnie.

I didn't talk to him much while I was there.

Myles missed his dad.

Truth is, I, too, drank and smoked through some of it, but Myles made that different for me. How can you escape when you simply can't escape?

Work.

I am an addict. I am addicted to work. The pace and flow of the kitchen. The tempo needed when the constant question is fight or flight.

This can look like a dark thing, a flaw, or it can look like a necessity. When you can't clock out at five and expect a paycheque, this is the reality of life. Every entrepreneur, small business owner, artist, working parent, anyone who has had to sacrifice to make work, to *create*, in order to put food on the table, you all know what is needed. And maybe you all know how it can end up being a kind of distraction, work becoming a comfort in itself.

Yet being with Myles all the time, staring at his beautiful face. That stuff about three-year-olds, Myles, if you ever read this, don't take it personally. You might have your own children one day and understand. Your face is sometimes the only thing that makes sense to me. My inspiration. My comfort. My answer. I looked at the face of my son, our son, and I just couldn't separate Johnnie from our lives. His face was in there too.

We talked on the phone. "How are you?" "How's it going?" "Any updates with the permits?"

A nervous tension and a taste of emptiness.

We both wanted to say more.

I flew back to Toronto. I saw Johnnie and we talked. I listened. He was honest and confessed to everything, how much he had been drinking and his addiction to cocaine. The building had issues, but the money had run out. Time had run out. We were in deep. "Death by a thousand cuts," he would say often.

He'd been jealous of my success, standing in the shadows.

We both tried to talk about what we'd lost, the stresses of parenting, the uncertainties, our fears. It was time to be honest.

Just standing back and looking at all we had been through was a good first step. We hadn't talked for so long, and talking meant so much. You're so busy with work, so busy with a toddler, there just is no time to talk.

Johnnie wanted to change. He went to Alcoholics Anonymous. He wanted us back, but I didn't know what I wanted. I didn't know if that trust could be rebuilt.

For a time he left the industry and found solace in construction as a general contractor.

It took me a while to stop blaming him for risking so much. Took a while for me to take some responsibility for being remote myself, watching him suffer and believing my own struggles were more important.

Mummy's voice came back to me in Florida. Two marriages, three kids. Blood of her Maroon grandmother. *Marriage isn't easy, so listen to your heart.*

I never imagined I would be a single mother, but I guess anything is possible.

It was during that visit to Plantation that I found the photo of my mum's first wedding. That joyless look in her eyes. Did I feel like that with Johnnie?

No.

Another quiet lesson from you, Nicey.

Johnnie stayed in Toronto and worked in construction while I lived with Myles in Prince Edward County. We saw each other on the weekends, but I wasn't ready to live with him again. Some customers from the Dinette invited me to revamp the menu of their restaurant in Picton, a town of the settled, of seekers, of hipsters, and, it turned out, a few racists. At a house they rented for me, and at the restaurant, I experienced some more than uncomfortable moments with people showing their own discomfort with me as a Black woman.

The owner of the B&B where I stayed for the first few days said I would probably be excited to meet the other Black person in town. Told me how much she liked Black men.

There was a history of bigotry and ignorance that lingered in the County. At least in my experience.

In the kitchen, music blaring on the speakers, the N-word being played by one of the chefs, a white boy. Kamoy, who had come with me to the County, asked if they could please turn it off because she was uncomfortable.

There were jealous and bitter recriminations toward me and my crew. We were the visitors stepping in, stepping on toes. We were the Black and Brown folks taking over. It all got poisoned.

A pretty shitty summer. But through it all, we helped put the restaurant, Sand and Pearl, on the map. Air Canada's *enRoute* magazine selected Sand and Pearl for their list of the best regional restaurants in Canada.

Over the years, in many ways, I've felt my role as a Black woman operating in white spaces is for the most part a challenge. The work I have to do to "fit in" feels overwhelming at times. Smile. Get it done. Adjust myself to make others feel like they don't have to adjust to me.

I was exhausted. Empty. I yearned for a purpose again, and I wanted my own space.

*Hibiscus.*
*Poinciana.*
*Lignum vitae.*
*Heliconia.*
*Blue mahoe.*
*Kiss-me-over-the-garden-gate.*
*Petals on the plates for the meals of lovers.*
*Stems from the graves of our parents.*

Johnnie and I got back together. Home was getting closer.

So many lessons over the years that prove something good will come from suffering and sacrifice . . . flowers from things that have died.

Myles and I headed back to Toronto, and Johnnie and I continued to work things out with each other.

I accepted a position as head chef at a brand-new brewpub in Leslieville, also in Toronto's East End. I thought about my connection to the British West Indies. Masala fish fry, puffed grains with blistered curry leaves. English pub fare, 1960s. It was a unique opportunity in a cool "art deco meets Scandinavian" space. We were combining an experimental brewery with a small-scale rooftop garden and nose-to-tail butchery program. My work was focused on creating an equitable back-of-house training program. I got on well with the owner, Mike, and some of my financial pressures were eased.

I also deepened my advocacy work. One of the first events I did was with Community Food Centres Canada and their Chefs for

Change dinner series. I cooked with a dozen other chefs to raise money to build vibrant spaces in low-income communities: community gardens, community kitchens, meal programs, and outreach programs. They had a mandate to bring people together to grow, cook, share, and advocate for good food for all. Fundraisers for Regent Park Community Food Centre followed, and I was a part of a fundraiser for the centre operating in Canada's oldest and largest social housing project. Black chefs were celebrated at FoodShare's annual fundraiser Recipe for Change, and I joined in there, too. A lot of similar opportunities came up, and I started to see myself as a change-maker as much as a chef.

Could I change societal structures through food and raise questions about inequities in restaurants? I talked about the position of Black chefs in Canada, recognizing that there were very few Black, female head chefs in the country. Why was that? How can we change that? I looked to other activist chefs in North America, Elle Simone, Mashama Bailey, Bryant Terry, Marcus Samuelsson, Kwame Onwuachi, and took inspiration from them.

I am so grateful for the many opportunities that came from our passion and hard work at Saturday Dinette. I had already appeared as a judge on *MasterChef Canada* and *Top Chef Canada*. And now I was a judge on a new show called *Wall of Chefs*. I am most proud to have been included in a documentary film called *The Heat: A Kitchen (R)evolution*, which looked at six female chefs in the world. An invitation came to travel to Korea to represent the film at the Seoul Eco Film Festival, and I fell in love with the city and Korean food. And I was asked to speak at the MAD Symposium in Copenhagen on the demands of owning a restaurant and being a parent. (Mad is Danish for food.) It was funny to be sought after as an expert when I felt like I was winging it every day, hustling, doing what I always did, which was work, put my head down, don't look back, keep moving.

I'd like to say the dark times were over and that all my lessons were learned, but life seems to be about learning the same lesson a few times.

Owners of a restaurant called True True Pizza hired Johnnie and me as consultants. The place wasn't doing well, and they wanted some fresh blood to make it profitable again. We took a look at the menu and the space. Way too many pizzas on offer, too many toppings, too complicated, and the decor didn't match the space at all. The building was super cool, storied, with an original lamppost out front in the oldest part of Toronto near St. Lawrence Market. It needed work—the whole concept did—and the owners were open to new ideas.

Could we do something like we did at the Dinette? Or even better?

As it evolved, the plan was for us not to be consultants but to have vested interests. My name was to be attached as chef. It ended up right there on the beautiful floor-to-ceiling glass we had installed: True True Diner: A Collaboration with Chef Suzanne Barr.

My own space, my own team again. This time I had sous-chefs and a manager, and Johnnie left his construction role to supervise and manage everything from new plumbing, electrical, windows, lights, seating, fridges, stoves, from the ground up to the never-ending sky. He received a comfortable salary and was looking after the day-to-day.

True True began in earnest. It's no small thing to set up a new restaurant and concept like that. The menu alone was six months in the making. I was eventually paid as head chef, with a salary much lower than what I made at my previous jobs, but I was in it for the long haul. A little sweat equity never hurt nobody—money and ownership would come later. Johnnie and I talked about future opportunities with our partners. We just needed to get this formula right, then wait for the possibilities to roll in.

All the ideas I had for equality at the Dinette, making my staff feel respected, paying them a living wage, encouraging them to feel they had a stake in the business—we set all that in motion. Respect. We did elaborate interviews with prospective staff and went through long sessions of training with them once they were hired. We shared tips, and there was no separation between the front and back of house. Some of our staff were new to Canada, and it was hugely important to us to make this feel like a safe space, a home away from home where they could learn about the restaurant business.

We did a soft launch, wanting a slow build and good word of mouth. The mayor of Toronto, John Tory, came by. Activist Paul Taylor, Chef Lynn Crawford, television host Noah Cappe. Chef Mark McEwan visited to eat our True True burger and country fried steak.

Like I said, new concepts take time. But from the beginning our partners, the landlords, were anxious about not enough money coming in. *Put fries on the menu. Pizzas.* Two worlds were colliding, and I didn't open my eyes to that fact.

We dusted off the photos from Saturday Dinette and put them on the walls at True True. Diners were some of the earliest restaurants, places to feed workers, set up near trains and transit to give people comfort and nourishment on their journeys—somewhere inside I felt that symbolic connection, on my journey, never still, looking for comfort before the next step. We tried to recreate the vibe and the food that we left behind at the Dinette, but our partners just couldn't get behind the concept.

I've always said to my team, "Make sure your story is on the plate." I fight for cultural representation in kitchens and menus. I like the challenges of creating new conversations—bringing something new to this space known mostly for pizza. A deep and beautiful trust can build when you make a name for yourself for quality—people will come along for the ride knowing that however different your creations might be, because they are yours they will be *good*.

The weekend brunch gave us our run. We had lines the moment the doors opened. We launched a dinner series called For the Love Of, with guest chefs: Chef Bashir Munye and Chef Adrian Forte. Magical nights leaving guests mesmerized through spoken word, through conversations about the power of Black chefs in kitchens.

It can be tiresome to listen to someone saying they worked hard, can't it? Repetitive for me to show that an endless string of fourteen-hour days can wear you down. Johnnie correcting the work of bad plumbers, meetings with staff, meetings with partners, both of us trying to be creative and joyful with our aprons on fire. All in the name of hope. One day, one day, the adequate money would come in.

We soon made it on *BlogTO* as best new brunch spot, got great attention on Post City's TRNTO, and we were shortlisted for *Toronto Life*'s best new restaurant 2020.

The lines were there and getting longer, but not long enough or fast enough for our partners. Money was what they cared about. And to some extent, I get it. Everyone needs to square away some cheese. But they were from a corporate real estate background, and they didn't share my dreams of slowly demonstrating quality, of building trust, of doing more than just selling covers.

The tough thing for me was that they were capitalizing on my brand. When my publicists were involved in marketing the restaurant, when the partners talked it up, it was my name that drove the story, my name on those windows. They sold my brand but never respected what that brand actually was—I stand up for people of colour, I want equality in the industry, and I want to advocate for silenced voices to have a presence and to tell their stories through food.

The storm gathered and blew across the world. In March 2020, the news was that a virus had settled in Toronto and things would change forever.

COVID-19 crippled our industry, took the lifeblood out of cities and the livelihoods of so many of my friends and heroes. We were scared, like everyone, at the beginning, but Johnnie and I drew up a plan to weather the storm. We looked into sources of funding and ways to keep our staff secure. I told our partners about government subsidies that we could draw on, and they said they would look into them.

I don't know if they pursued them, but we never saw any of those funds.

No restaurant. No customers.

What the pandemic revealed was a gross inequity between land-lords and the people who paid their rent. The people who give a city colour are the ones with imaginations and something to sell, not the people who tax that creativity. But the landlords got the bailouts and relief, kept their right to make money while their tenants were told that their businesses had to close.

I worked with a few food justice programs in the city that were feeding the most vulnerable people. I had a huge kitchen and food that couldn't go to waste. We prepared care packages for our staff and scheduled safe pick-up time slots for them to come through. As I sat at home watching way too much social media, I thought, why not get engaged and start hosting cooking classes online? Requests came in for quarantine cooking, and I posted recipes in several publications. Partnership and endorsement opportunities came in for me and True True Diner—even Myles, and I took to Twitch with him as my sous-chef.

I hosted a hip-hop Sunday brunch making biscuits on True True's Instagram feed, and we hosted a few Zoom sessions with our True True staff, reassuring them that we would be open as soon as we had clearance from the government. It was important to keep the brand alive in the city. True True would be reopening with some new and exciting offerings. I began recipe testing and recipe devel-opment with Johnnie. We created a new menu offering to-go items, baked goods, and commissary kitchen fare. We held meetings every other week in the beginning to share our progress and what our pivots could look like.

No restaurant. No customers.

Our partners pulled the plug.

# True True Diner

Last fall, after months of hard work, excitement, and anticipation, we opened the doors to True True Diner. It became a go-to for people looking for familiar vibes and Afro-Caribbean soulful comfort food. It was a hub where we celebrated and lifted Black chefs and others who deserved to be seen. We chose to open as a diner to honour all the civil rights sit-ins that happened in diners across North America and helped shape Black history. And today, it is with a heavy heart that I have to share—True True Diner is officially closed.

We had temporarily closed at the start of the pandemic in March as did many restaurants with the hopes of reopening, but now this will never happen. The story behind what happened and who was involved is still a private matter, but I want to speak to the bigger picture which I see clearly now. Unbeknownst to me, True True Diner never had a fighting chance. I am not just speaking to my business. I am calling out the injustices that continue to plague Black- and Indigenous-owned and operated businesses.

It became a safe place for so many of my staff who are newcomers to this country. This was for some their first job in Canada, and it's an honour to call them family. Hard work, social justice, having a dream . . .

Our small businesses are no match for the toxic and biased systemic structures that can legally and quite easily dismiss everything we've worked so hard to build. We didn't want to close our doors. The decision was made for us by partners who kept us in the dark.

We wanted to keep going, and keep growing, and our staff were on board. Our customers were on board. We'd made plans for a post-COVID-19 restaurant; however, were not given a chance to succeed.

This theft of power is shared by so many folks that look like me. My partners, like many landowners and landlords, don't understand the magnitude and importance of our country's Black- and Indigenous-owned businesses. Prior to the pandemic, as a Black-owned, female-operated venue in the heart of Toronto, True True Diner preached and practiced strong social programs supporting youth, students, newcomers, and chefs of colour. We paid above minimum wage and practiced equal pay for equal work. Yet, during the pandemic struggles, our white privileged partners were eligible for a big slice of that handout pie and never offered us a bite. We tried so hard to keep this business going with pitched plans of innovative and meaningful pivots.

We wanted to keep it going to support our extended family of staff and customers and to continue the work that became so crucial to our community, including advocating for fair and just rights for Black, Indigenous and people of colour while also advancing opportunities for people with visible and invisible disabilities.

Food security and accessibility. Equal pay. Creating safe spaces. Championing mental health within our industry. And so much more . . .

I am NOT defeated. I am taking back my power. This is a call to action to all our brothers and sisters and allies. Contact your local governments and call out these injustices. Support all Black, Indigenous, POC, and LGBTQ businesses. Call out companies that use and abuse corporate law and financial institution gains. Although True True Diner is closed, this is just the beginning. The TRUTH will never be closed. #BlackLivesMatter

Just as it was starting to grow, six months from the beginning, it was over before it even began.

It's the Dinette over again but different this time. And I ask this question:

Why can't this girl keep a restaurant?

Sitting on a beach with my dying mother. How can I keep the things I love?

# SIX

# RITE OF PASSAGE

New broom sweep clean, but owl broom noe dem cahna

L et me take you back to the Gladstone Hotel. Come in and have a drink.

It's two years prior and I'm creating a menu that means more to me than any other.

*I stand here now as your daughter, a sister, and a mother*

One of my customers from the Dinette was Christina Zeidler, who owned the Gladstone Hotel. Part of the Gladstone's identity was to have an artist-in-residence, and Christina had the idea of having a chef-in-residence as well. She wanted me to inaugurate the tradition. She loved the Dinette and suggested I do a Dinette-like brunch with all the fixings, all the things that our customers loved: shrooms on toast, trout hash, grits, buckwheat pancakes. You know the drill.

I was emotionally done with it. It made me feel sick to my stomach. I just couldn't do it.

The hardest question for an artist can sometimes be: *Why?* When you've lost something, when a project hasn't worked out, when hard work has led to nothing, you ask yourself that question: *Why am I doing this?* It's easy to answer questions about what you're doing—I'm cooking—but answering the why . . . Why do you cook for nothing, why do you cook till your feet bleed, sixteen hours a day, for a shitty review, for no review, for a landlord blackening the sky like a vampire.

Sometimes you can't answer the other questions properly without asking yourself why. *What am I going to do next?* First I need to be honest about why I am doing it at all.

Why do I cook?

I wanted to make a statement about who I was.

When I told Johnnie I didn't know what to make at the Gladstone, he said, *Think about your mum. Think about Jamaica. Think about your kitchen in your parents' house growing up. You need to talk about those things.* And by talking, he meant cooking.

Now, I'd be lying if I said I had any clarity at that point in my life—I was in that blur of motherhood and marital collapse, wondering what the fuck. But Johnnie's suggestion hit me somewhere deep, and I can see now that it did because it partly answered that question of why. Why do I cook? I cook because I want to make my beautiful mother better. I believe food is healing. I want to feel how food connects me to my past. I want to connect with my parents, my grandparents through food.

The plate is my canvas. I cook because I'm good at it, and I love how food makes me feel. The fat girl that sleeps within me remembers being criticized for my love of food as a girl. I felt shame for loving food, but the food loved me deeply—it made me feel good despite harsh words and judgments. The sweetness from the roast, the salty notes inviting thirst, and the things that I can drink to wash it down. I feel alive in the kitchen. I dream of the process of creating a dish that begins as I close my eyes, heart beating, shapes colliding, colours, shades, texture, and smell. I cook because it connects me to my mother. I feel alive controlling the pans as I dance on the line. I live to cook.

"I want to go back to where I grew up."

That was Nicey talking to me when I was twenty-two.

Before her official diagnosis, when my mum was suffering from back pain, she said she wanted to see Jamaica again. We'd been back as a family—that short trip to visit my cousins—and she and my father had taken a cruise around the island, but she hadn't been back home, to Saint Elizabeth Parish, since she was thirteen.

So she and I went together. We went upcountry to the parish, along winding roads with these monster trucks approaching. I closed my eyes not knowing if I would live or die until they passed and honked their horns. You had to know your way around to drive those streets.

Familiar but unfamiliar, that's how things were appearing to me. Not memories of a place I had actually been to, but of a place I felt. Smell of sea, mango tree, and jungle sweat. The city sounds in Kingston had been *loud*. The city had a pulse, but here some other pulse was beating.

Sheep, goats, hogs, and horses, sugar cane, peas, ginger, and tobacco. Smells I could feel on my skin. Clouds over the mountains emptied and regathered while the sun kept shining. My great grand-mother, a Maroon, lived in those mountains, descendant of escaped slaves. I could feel her waist-deep and nourished by this place, while the invaders and the hungry were coming from other places to find gold and wonder. I was too old to believe in paradise or Eden, but my senses were coming alive to a place I'd known but never been to.

My mum was excited and nervous, overwhelmed with so many emotions. We pulled up to a simple country house, a patio lined with tiles that helped keep you cool in the night. Country dogs ran up to the car.

I was a North American girl. My first thoughts were, *Is there air conditioning? How bad are the mosquitos at night?*

I had a couple of big realizations that started growing on that trip. I was still young, not a cook yet, but I felt later that these were moments that formed me. One was just how simple my mum's beginnings were.

We took a day trip to her house, through lush and sticky woods. It was hard for her to find at first. We pulled up to the house, her grandmother's house, and saw a tiny, dilapidated place, the roof knocked in, empty. As soon as we got out of the car, we heard a woman's voice say *Nicey?* Truth. As soon as our feet touched the ground. A neighbour recognized her and came over to see where she'd been. Forty years had passed, and she knew her immediately.

She told us that all our family had gone. There wasn't a Facey left.

I remember a kind of breathlessness when I heard that. As if some kind of claim or opportunity had been lost.

This parish so green. Mummy told me stories. How they walked for two days to the city. How they went to the river to trade goods. They all slept on the ground in the house and buried the dead in the backyard. When she was a baby, her siblings put her down on one of the graves and her eyes rolled back. They thought it was a duppy—a spirit, possessed.

We went down to the river, the Black River, known for its peppa shrimp. Undeveloped, unmanicured. So beautiful, even with debris and paper plates in the banks. Imagine what it felt like at night, the music bumping and people dancing, big speakers rolling out on the back of pickup trucks. Not simple, nothing is simple, but some-how honest. Something spoke to me, a feeling in my blood.

That's why that breathlessness when I heard the old woman say the Faceys were all gone. The two of us, my mum and me, we both wanted something back.

It's easy to romanticize or over-sensualize Jamaica. Astonishing beauty, lush country, rich culture, hedonism itself becoming a brand there. But there are areas of unimaginable poverty, isolation, misogyny, and bigotry, and it's a poster child of colonization—culture lost, way of life lost, riches gained at all kinds of cost. Was I a colonizer myself, a North American tourist getting romanced by these sights and stories, even though my ancestors and my family were buried here?

My mum knew joy in that one-room house. I felt it in all her stories, and the stories her brother told of her later. She told me how good she felt coming home from school, describing her grandma, who looked after her, tall and statuesque, wearing mili-tary boots but being fair. This was her refuge, the place she could look back on all her life and say, *That was home.*

I went for a walk on my own, and a man in a shack was making a very traditional dish called bammy—grated cassava that had been through a machine, and then compacted into pucks to be fried in oil until golden brown. Salted. It was an accompaniment for fish or meat, or eaten alone. I had my camera (which I always did) and I asked if I could take some photos of the bammy he was going to sell in the city. The whites of his eyes were so white, his skin blue-black. He lived a hard life, a country life, a slow life. Never left Jamaica. Didn't smile. A hard labourer. As the shredding started, dust covered his hand in speckles on his skin. I saw the real rawness of this man, of the cassava, the spirit of the parish.

I wanted to connect Jamaica and Canada. Why? What I realized about Jamaica was that while I hadn't experienced much of it, I knew its salt and sweetness. I had eaten it all my life. My mum's yearning for home, my own yearning for my mum—all our experiences and heartbreak that made us want something that wasn't quite there—we could all come home and find satisfaction in food.

At the Gladstone, I staked my claim. I brought the Faceys back to the parish. I honoured my mum and her history.

I had seen and been inspired by menus written by Alice Waters of Chez Panisse, and Dominique Crenn of Atelier Crenn, which took the form of letters. Crenn used poetry to narrate the experience in her dining room—each line of a poem was associated with a dish, and you ate with the poetry in your head. I was in awe of the intimacy that created, the sensual layering of words and flavours. For the first time I saw a menu as a tool, another kitchen tool—you can tell a story with it, say things.

And what did I want to say?

I hadn't talked about my mum. I talked *to* her sometimes, in my head, but I hadn't really addressed for myself the grief I felt from her loss. I'd been running, hustling, trying to get my life going.

I felt guilt about the way she died, guilt about my role as her daughter. I hadn't asked enough questions when she was alive. Had I given back any of the comfort I got from her?

I wished she could meet my son.

So I wrote her a letter, and in between thoughts, in between moments, I tried, as proudly as I could, to recreate Jamaica. I wanted to tell her who I'd become. How much we all missed her and loved her. I wanted her to be good to Daddy. Forgiveness. The food would talk about the journey for so many Jamaicans crossing that Atlantic, an invitation from the Queen. Forced labour. Stolen lands. Jamaica's riches. The story of the people, the traditions shared between the many Caribbean islands. I called it Rite of Passage because it felt like creating the menu brought me to a new stage in my life. I was becoming a daughter to my mother in a way I hadn't before.

Food that was eaten from a take-out container—that's how a lot of Jamaican cooking was seen. Obviously I ate it at home, but I rarely went to restaurants to eat it. As a chef I wasn't trained to make it. But once I made the decision to create an authentically Jamaican menu, one that was my own, the dishes started flowing.

Ackee Terrine

Jerk Chicken Ramen

Red Lentil–Stuffed Plantains

Banana Leaf Steamed Fish

Black Cake

I transformed plut, a cook-up or stew that Maroons used to make from the vegetables that grew around them as they hid. Thinking of my great-grandmother, I transformed plut into a burger. A veggie burger full of roasted squash, fresh green peas, shredded raw beets. I made it according to Rastafarian Ital principles, and I made it vital. My hands in prayer at my chest, thinking of all the men and women who came before me.

Dear Mummy,

As I daydream about my fondest memories of you my eyes fill with joy. I know and remember the woman you were and now I understand the challenges you faced. I stand here now as your daughter, a sister and a mother thankful to tell you that we are all ok! Daddy is doing well, still making the classics:

| Grilled jerk chicken ramen \| pineapple sofrito \| soft poached quail egg \| black garlic oil | 21 |
| Coconut turmeric trotters \| charred sugar cane \| chicharron \| highland blue | 17 |
| Roucou braised goat shoulder \| mint daikon green mango slaw | 24 |

I remember Sundays as our family day—working in the garden, washing the car, eating breakfast with Tanya and you making dinner. Ackee and saltfish were my favorite but man we were in for a treat when you got your hands on callaloo:

**(V)** avail.  Ackee terrine \| salted cod \| pickled onions + blueberries \| festival \| tomato consomme  —  22

**(VG)** avail.  Callaloo fried rice \| coconut \| beef liver \| pickled garlic \| pigeon peas  —  19

The many memories we shared as a family were so enriched with cooking and eating together. I remember when we would ask daddy to make patties—it was a true family affair:

Daily patties \| gravy \| coconut lime chutney  —  14

There is so much I want to tell you about my life and the woman I have become. The sacrifices that you had to make in your life impacted the woman I came to be. Myles is my son who is now two years old—he loves eating, playing any sport, reading and is full of so much life. As I watch over him from a distance he reminds me of myself when you would cook plantains in the kitchen and I would try and eat them up the moment they came out of the pan:

**(V) (GF)**  Red lentil stuffed plantains \| lion cheese \| cassava chips \| pickleys  —  16

Myles is a handful but such an inspiration to life as a mother, a wife and a working chef. I married an incredible person whom is my life partner and keeps us together as a family much like how you did with ours:

**(V) (GF)** avail.  Plut burger \| lion cheese \| shitake bacon \| toasted coco bread \| pickled mango \| callaloo  —  18.50

I remember Sunday dinners meaning so much to you because it was a day we slowed down and ate together on the "guest only" dining table using the wedding cutlery and eyelet white lace tablecloth. It was our evening to celebrate the feast you'd prepared with all the fixins. The salad would literally have ten different ingredients at least two would be fruit:

**(VG) (GF)** avail.  Junkanoo savoy slaw \| papaya + mango citrus water \| mint labneh \| s + p crumble  —  9

The Sunday feasts were your way of showing us your past, growing up in a small village in St. Elizabeth, Jamaica. The land and rivers were rich in bauxite and welcomed a beautiful harvest of plump juicy mangos, ripe breadfruit, and a plethora of seafood:

Banana leaf steamed fish \| provisions + gravy \| pickled mango \| fish tea  —  32

You were the third eldest and the only one that left home to start your own family in another country. It must have been hard to leave your siblings, friends and your mother. I know grandma was the rock of our family raising eight children, praying for them and wishing for the best future for us all. The stories I'm now told about you being a fierce dancer, an inspiring older sister and a talented artist in your own right makes me so proud and honoured to call you my mother.

Thank you for always smiling, laughing and pushing me, Wayne and Tanya to be the best at whatever it is we wanted to be. You left us with so many gifts and memories of the life you created in Florida and the life you left behind in Jamaica—a beautiful island rich of flavors, smells, culture and people:

**(V) (GF)**  Chilled coconut soup \| coconut lime chutney \| irish moss \| fennel fronds  —  10

I love you and miss you dearly. Thank you for the life you shared and the countless memories we will always keep.

With love,

*Sharaye*

(VG) \| vegetarian    (V) \| vegan    (GF) \| gluten free    avail. \| modification available

I put on Jimmy Cliff, Maxi Priest, Sister Nancy, De La Soul, Toots and the Maytals, Marvin Gaye, Stevie Wonder, the Beatles. Music that my mother loved. Mesmerized on the dancefloor. Spinning. Spinning. Spinning.

Sundays.

The family day.

Working in our garden, and you made us dinner, how we were in for a treat when you got your hands on callaloo.

I finally had a chance to mourn.

When you see the charcoal next to the pig knuckle, you see the colour of the people who were given these offal meats, and you taste how they transformed them. Their skin. Our skin. Our story. Their story.

Curry was the colour of the country. The richness in the soil. Yellow, green, and black, Jamaica's national colours. Rice and peas with my mum's favourite liver and onions, giving us the iron and the nutrients. Jungle-green callaloo, bitter and nutty.

The final piece—the Black Cake—a little offering. A thank you. You eat it at a wedding and take it back home with you, some sweetness to remind you of the day. Of the love. A brief moment.

When di yardies came to the Gladstone, I was nervous at first. *This isn't ackee and saltfish!*

But they tried it and said, *This is different*. I said, *Different is good*.

My happiest memories of those raw, dark times, shortly after the Dinette closed, with all those storms still to come, was being told that customers wanted to meet the chef. People had read the letter to my mum. They tried this food from all over the map, centred in Jamaica, and they wanted to embrace me, to tell me they loved it. Sometimes they were crying.

I think of my mum in every season, but there's an image of her on a white sand beach that is as clear to me today as if it happened yesterday.

Two months before she died, five of my family members rented a van and drove from Plantation to the northern part of Florida, near the border with Alabama.

We had learned that her cancer was back and she made the decision not to go through chemotherapy again. The cancer was in her spine and was travelling to her brain; the prognosis was dire. Chemo would possibly prolong her life, but the side effects were just too much for her.

We'd heard about a clinic in Northern Florida that specialized in Eastern medicine, and we hoped that they might have more natural ways to ease her pain. We rented a passenger van and drove eleven hours north. Mummy was frail and quiet, and we realized halfway through that we should have taken a plane. It pained her body to sit upright in the van, although we tried to make her as comfortable as we could with pillows and blankets. That night we had to stop at a hospital and we slept in the empty waiting room. They gave her some fluids through an IV and an oxygen tank, which we rolled out of the emergency room to the van in the morning.

We finally arrived at the clinic.

Wind chimes. Tranquillity waterfall. Cream-coloured walls.

We sat with the doctors in a dimly lit room filled with leafy ferns and bonsai trees. My mum seemed calm, although her skin was pale and her head hung forward as if too heavy for her neck. I still saw a spark in her eyes when she looked over at me, the doctors telling her gently that they couldn't cure her cancer, but they would help her manage her pain and try to strengthen her body using traditional medicines. We left the room with teas, tinctures, some hope.

My first memory of Florida is going to the beach. I'm five years old in Fort Lauderdale. The waves are huge and mesmerizing, and everyone is happy. My mum is in a polka-dot bikini, and me and Tanya walk along the shore with our feet in the salt water. I like looking back to see how our footprints fill with water, and then disappear. I don't like sand on my towel, so Tanya shakes it off for me and I sit down with her to play with shovels and a bucket. Wayne playing in the water. My parents are on their backs, eyes closed, and the sun feels warm on my shoulders.

In the van, heading back to Plantation, we saw a sign for Destin Beach. Mummy wanted to see the ocean, so we followed the signs to the water. It was a few miles south of the I-10, and the road eventually led to a bridge that connected a long spit of land to the mainland. The beach was snuggled against the emerald Gulf of Mexico.

*I'll carry her*, my uncle said.

My mum's body light as a child's. Wrapped in a blanket, sunglasses protecting her eyes from the brightness, she was limp in my uncle's arms. Sand so fine it squeaked underfoot like the first snow on cold days in Toronto.

When we reached the water, we took off her shoes and held her arms as she stood on the sand. Waves talked quietly around her ankles. I think we all knew that this would be her last visit to a beach. She was fifty-six years old.

Roll out waves and come back.

Take our stories and tell them.

There are so many things I want to do.

I'm not stopping.

I hang those photos of civil rights heroes in my restaurants because they inspire me. They remind me that this life is a gift; nurture it. I want to make a contribution. If I can hold on to just a little of their courage, a spark of their flame, keep it burning in the kitchen.

Feed people who need it. Feed their souls. Fight for workers' rights in the hospitality trade. Fix what's broken. Pave a new path. Let's level this field. Women's stories matter. Black women's stories matter. Fair and equal pay to all. A fight for mental health. BIPOC farmers want their land back.

I'll keep moving, but it's good to slow down and remember.

Every immigrant's story, maybe every human story, is about adaptation, trying to make a mark in a new place, finding familiar people and making new friends. Listening and hearing your voice. Wondering who you are when you've lost your home, and building a new home with wonder, with struggle.

I'm in Toronto now. Who knows where I'll be in the future?

This city is where so many stories like mine have played out, apartment buildings, homes, rooming houses, kitchen walls full of stories from elsewhere.

I think of Sonny and Nicey walking these streets. Bathurst—Blackhurst—sounds of rock-steady music from Jamaica in some of the shops and clubs—Jackie Mittoo, the Sheiks, Wayne McGhie. It's not quite ska, not quite reggae, not soul or funk, but a mixture of it all, the musicians figuring it out.

Sonny's twenty-two years old in the fall of 1965. He rents a room in a boarding house for twenty dollars a week, kicked out of his friend Hubert's house by Hubert's wife only three days after arriving from Jamaica. He's making $1.35 an hour, and the first thing he buys is a record player. Eats oxtail and fish in Kensington Market, and chicken in a basket. Hair done crisp by an Italian named Solomon. Girls can't keep away.

"What's going on? I haven't seen you around here. You look good in purple."

He asks her to have lunch one time. She brushes him off, makes it tough for him.

She works at Loomis & Toles art shop, and sees him out there now for weeks.

She has a spirit, wants to make people comfortable, says her friend Ivy. She's quiet and wants to learn. Sonny drives taxis. He'll open a flower shop and get a job at a printing company. Years later, he'll want to open a patty shop where Jamaican old-timers could come and play dominoes.

Sonny and Nicey ate patties in Toronto, said things only they would ever know. Remember.

See him walking out front there for weeks, wanting to have lunch.

Caught her eye.

He'll catch her heart.

# EPILOGUE

Toronto has been home to Johnnie, Myles, and me for almost eight years.

I'm living there now, but I'm not sure for how long. Like it was for my parents, my life in Toronto has been a constant hustle; we're always trying to find a way to make ends meet while discovering things about ourselves. As the city gets more and more expensive, and the possibility of buying a house, escaping landlords, becomes further from reality, Johnnie and I think of other options. Florida, Europe, Australia.

Right now, I'm doing demos online, cooking mushroom tempura sliders and Jamaican salt cod fritters.

I know I'll be back in a restaurant one day. I know I can create change.

I want to tell Myles to embrace all his memories, the bad ones and good. Try not to run away.

We have a home now, see. No matter where it is. The three of us in a kitchen. If we're together, we can be anywhere, hands around a bowl. I'll cook the moments that make us.

# RECIPES

Likkle More

# Welcoming Seeds   *Makes about 3 cups (750 mL)*

*Sometimes the welcome can be about surprise as much as comfort. You find a home in a place you least expect. In Kauai, at Blossoming Lotus, every table is given a bowl of these seeds as a greeting. Licorice. Salt. A hint of caramel. A mixture of flavours releasing sweetness and umami in perfect balance. I added the macadamia nuts as a way to honour Hawaii, one of my favourite places on earth. These seeds and nuts open the palate, and eating a handful brings me right back to the deep green beauty of Kapa'a. Enjoy Welcoming Seeds on their own or on top of a salad.*

1 tablespoon (15 mL) fennel seeds

2 cups (500 mL) raw pepitas or pumpkin seeds

1 cup (250 mL) macadamia nuts

2 tablespoons (30 mL) pure maple syrup

2 tablespoons (30 mL) tamari

¼ teaspoon (1 mL) ground cayenne pepper

2 teaspoons (10 mL) raw sesame seeds

½ teaspoon (2 mL) sea salt

Preheat the oven to 300°F (150°C). Line a baking sheet with parchment paper.

In a dry medium skillet over high heat, lightly toast the fennel seeds until fragrant, about 1 minute. Transfer to a mortar or spice grinder and lightly grind the seeds.

In a large bowl, place the crushed fennel seeds, pepitas, macadamia nuts, maple syrup, tamari, and cayenne. Toss until the seeds and nuts are evenly coated in the liquid.

Spread the seed and nut mixture in an even layer on the prepared baking sheet. Bake for 10 minutes. Remove the baking sheet from the oven and lightly toss the mixture, moving the nuts and seeds in the middle of the baking sheet toward the outside and vice versa. Bake for an additional 8 to 10 minutes, or until evenly browned and toasted.

As soon as you remove the Welcoming Seeds from the oven, sprinkle with the sesame seeds and salt. Toss to combine. Add more salt if desired. Let cool before serving.

Leftover Welcoming Seeds can be stored in an airtight container at room temperature for up to 14 days.

# Chilled Coconut Soup with Lime Coconut Compote    Serves 4 to 6

*The taste of seawater on your lips. The smell of pimento wood being readied in the fire.*
*The coconuts are ripe. Crack one on a rock and use the shell to scrape the flesh. This*
*soup celebrates history, culture, and the simplicity of the coconut: fruit, nut, and seed.*
*It combines land and sea—dried sea moss is one of the main ingredients. It's the*
*perfect soup for a hot, humid afternoon. The tanginess of the lime compote will quench*
*your thirst. Sweet. Nutty. Creamy. Decadent. Serve it in a coconut shell.*

### Coconut Soup

1 cup (250 mL) dried sea moss

3 young green Thai coconuts

2 scallions, ends trimmed

2 cups (500 mL) canned coconut milk

1 whole yellow Scotch bonnet pepper

1 clove garlic

1 teaspoon (5 mL) sea salt

½ teaspoon (2 mL) pure liquid honey

White pepper

### Lime Coconut Compote

1 brown-skinned coconut, cracked into 4 pieces

1 teaspoon (5 mL) lime zest

2 tablespoons (30 mL) fresh lime juice

2 tablespoons (30 mL) coconut cream

1 teaspoon (5 mL) coconut vinegar

Pinch of sea salt

### Garnishes (optional)

Chili oil

Fresh chives

**Start the Coconut Soup** Place the sea moss in a medium bowl and cover with water.
Massage the moss to loosen any debris. Drain. Repeat until all the debris has been
washed away. Cover the moss with 2 to 3 cups (500 to 750 mL) of filtered water, making
sure all of the moss is submerged. Let stand on the counter overnight.    *continued . . .*

Drain the sea moss and place it in the jar of a high speed blender. Add ½ cup (125 mL) filtered water. Blend until smooth, adding an additional 1 to 2 tablespoons (15 to 30 mL) water if necessary to create a smooth mixture. Transfer to an airtight container. Cover and place it in the fridge for at least 2 hours to thicken.

Carefully use a machete or large kitchen knife to take off the top of each green coconut. Pour the coconut water into a medium bowl or container and set aside. Carefully crack the coconuts in half lengthwise. Use a spoon to scoop out 2 cups (500 mL) of the coconut flesh. Place it in a medium bowl and set aside.

Line a small plate with paper towels. Fill a medium bowl with ice water. Fill a small saucepan with water and bring it to a boil. Drop the scallions into the boiling water and cook for 10 to 15 seconds. Use tongs to remove the scallions from the pot and immediately place them in the ice water to stop the cooking. After 3 to 5 seconds, transfer the scallions to the paper towel–lined plate.

In a medium saucepan over medium-high heat, combine the coconut milk, Scotch bonnet, garlic, salt, honey, and pepper to taste. Bring to a boil. Reduce the heat to medium and let simmer for about 15 to 20 minutes, until the mixture reduces by about half. Use a fine-mesh sieve to strain the solids from the mixture. Let cool.

**Make the Lime Coconut Compote** Use the zesting side of box grater to shred the coconut pulp, making 1 cup (250 mL) of shredded pulp. Wrap the shredded coconut in a piece of cheesecloth and squeeze out any excess coconut milk, adding it to the bowl with the green coconut water.

Place the shredded coconut in a clean small bowl. Add the lime zest and juice, coconut cream, and salt. Stir to combine. Set aside.

**Finish the Coconut Soup** Place the green coconut flesh, sea moss mixture, coconut vinegar, scallions, and coconut milk mixture in the jar of a blender. Blend on low speed. Gradually stream in all of the green coconut water until the mixture is smooth and creamy. Season with salt and white pepper, to taste.

Divide the soup among bowls. Add a scoop of the lime coconut compote to each serving and garnish with chili oil and chives (if using).

# Scotch Bonnet Tomato Consommé *Serves 6*

*This dish can be served as a starter or a palate cleanser or with Festival Dumplings (page 198) for lunch, but it's particularly wonderful served alongside my Ackee Terrine with Whipped Coconut Salt Cod (page 202). Traditionally, chopped tomatoes are added to ackee and saltfish for their sweet acidity. This broth is a refreshing mash-up of sweet Roma tomatoes and Scotch bonnet peppers.*

1 pound (450 g) ripe Roma tomatoes,
  cut into quarters
2 scallions with ends trimmed, cut into thirds
1 tablespoon (15 mL) fresh thyme leaves
1 teaspoon (5 mL) coarsely chopped red Scotch bonnet pepper
1 tablespoon (15 mL) extra-virgin olive oil
2 teaspoons (10 mL) sea salt, divided
3 tablespoon (45 mL) coconut liquid aminos

Preheat the oven to 375°F (190°C). Line a baking sheet with parchment paper.

Place the tomatoes in a large bowl. Add the scallions, thyme, and Scotch bonnet. Toss to combine. Add the olive oil and 1 teaspoon (5 mL) of salt and toss until evenly coated. Spread the tomato mixture in an even layer on the prepared baking sheet and cover with foil. Roast for 20 minutes. Remove the foil from the baking sheet and roast for an additional 15 minutes, until the tomatoes are caramelized. Let cool.

Transfer the roasted tomato mixture to a high-speed blender. Add the coconut liquid aminos and 1 cup (250 mL) of water and blend until smooth. Line a fine-mesh sieve with two layers of cheesecloth and place it over a medium bowl. Pour the tomato purée into the lined sieve and gently fold the cheesecloth on top of the purée. Allow to strain in the fridge overnight.

Discard the solids remaining in the cheesecloth. Season the consommé with the remaining 1 teaspoon (5 mL) of salt.

Divide the consommé among small bowls. Optionally, serve with the Ackee Terrine with Whipped Coconut Salt Cod or with Festival Dumplings.

# Rosemary Socca  *Makes 4 pancakes*

*Standing in line with Johnnie on the cobblestone street outside our apartment in the*
*city centre of Nice, we waited for socca. Chickpea flour, water, and oil poured onto*
*a wide skillet and cooked on an open fire. Sprinkle of salt. Served on a paper plate.*
*The nuttiness from the chickpeas, crunchy salt, the purest olive oil had me on tilt.*
*Oil soaked the paper plate as we stood in the warm sun, not checking the time, just*
*enjoying. It's a vegan and gluten-free combination of pancake, crêpe, and dosa, and*
*we made our own version at Saturday Dinette. We added a hint of rosemary and served*
*it rolled, stuffed with lavender ricotta, and dusted with confectioners' sugar with*
*a drizzle of olive oil to finish it. I only wish we could have served it on paper plates.*

4 cups (1 L) chickpea flour

4 cups (1 L) water

⅓ cup (75 mL) extra-virgin olive oil,
    plus more for greasing the skillet

1 tablespoon (15 mL) sea salt

2 teaspoons (10 mL) chopped fresh rosemary

Flaky sea salt

Full-fat ricotta cheese (optional)

A glass of rosé wine (optional)

In a large bowl, add the chickpea flour, water, olive oil, salt, and rosemary. Stir to combine. You should be left with a thick batter resembling pancake batter. Cover and chill for 30 minutes in the fridge.

Preheat the broiler to high. Generously grease the bottom of a 12-inch (30 cm) oven-safe skillet or cast-iron pan with olive oil. Place it in the oven and allow it to heat up until almost smoking, about 6 minutes. Using a ladle, place 1½ cups (375 mL) of the batter into the pan and swirl it around. Use a spoon to help you smooth the batter out until it covers the bottom of the pan. Broil for 4 to 5 minutes, until golden and crispy. Slide the pancake onto a clean plate and repeat with the remaining batter.

Before serving, garnish each piece of socca with a sprinkle of sea salt and a dollop of ricotta, if using. Enjoy with a glass of rosé wine to complete the experience.

# Festival Dumplings  *Makes 12 dumplings*

*I can still remember my mum's hands gently kneading the dough for dumplings in her red mixing bowl. She was cooking up some magic. Making dumplings is a true rite of passage when learning to cook Caribbean cuisine. Festival Dumplings are the shape of a sausage, and they are fried until golden brown. Sweet and comforting. Dip them into Scotch Bonnet Tomato Consommé (page 195), then take a bite of my Ackee Terrine with Whipped Coconut Salt Cod (page 202). All together, these components make for a powerful punch of flavour. Dumplings are also delicious served with any kind of fried fish, jerk pork, or chicken, or with some mango chutney.*

2¼ cups (560 mL) all-purpose flour

¾ cup (175 mL) medium-grind cornmeal

3 tablespoons (45 mL) granulated sugar

1 tablespoon (15 mL) baking powder

¾ teaspoon (4 mL) salt

½ teaspoon (2 mL) freshly grated nutmeg

2 to 3 tablespoons (30 to 45 mL) salted butter, softened

1 cup (250 mL) buttermilk

4 cups (1 L) canola or vegetable oil

In a large bowl, whisk the flour, cornmeal, sugar, baking powder, salt, and nutmeg. Add the butter. Use your hands to work it into the flour mixture for about 1 minute, taking care not to overmix.

Make a well in the centre of the flour mixture and pour the buttermilk into it. Stir a few times with a wooden spoon until a loose dough forms. Turn the loose dough out onto a floured flat surface and knead for about 1 minute, until a soft smooth dough forms. Divide the dough into 12 equal pieces and place them on a tray or board. Cover with plastic wrap and let rest for 15 minutes.

Roll each piece of dough into the shape of a sausage about 2 inches (5 cm) in diameter.

Line a plate with paper towels. Place the oil in a large saucepan over medium heat. Bring the oil to a temperature of 350°F (180°C).

Use a slotted spoon to carefully place 3 dumplings into the oil. Fry in the shallow oil for about 4 minutes, until golden brown, making sure to turn the dumplings frequently so they brown on all sides. Use a slotted spoon to transfer the dumplings to the paper towel–lined plate and let drain. Repeat until all of the dumplings have been fried. Let cool for a few minutes and serve warm.

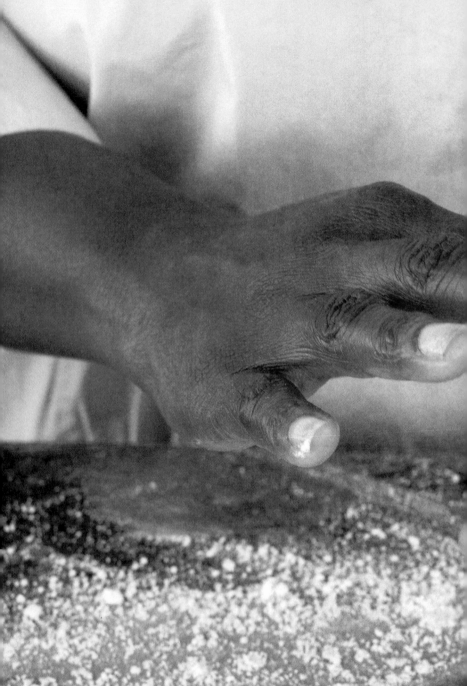

# Ackee Terrine with Whipped Coconut Salt Cod Serves 6

*The red pod of the ackee fruit holds the golden nugget. Succulent joy. Tanya and I would stand on stools at the counter cleaning the fruit, trying to keep the shape of the flesh while we separated it from the shiny black seed. This recipe celebrates the traditional Jamaican dish of ackee and saltfish, but I've given it my own spin. When I make it, I can feel my mother dancing on the kitchen tiles beside me. Her absence still devastates me. She was my best friend. Her love for her family showed when she stepped into the kitchen. I'm trying to keep up that tradition.*

*I made this dish at the Gladstone Hotel and served it along with my Scotch Bonnet Tomato Consommé (page 195) and Festival Dumplings (page 198) as a way to celebrate the classic dish. Fresh ackee is hard to find in North America, so I use the canned version.*

### Ackee Terrine

3 cans (19 ounces/540 mL each) ackee, drained

1 tablespoon (15 mL) extra-virgin olive oil

1 small red onion, diced

2 teaspoons (10 mL) fresh thyme leaves, divided

½ teaspoon (2 mL) sea salt

2 cups (500 mL) water

¼ cup (60 mL) gelatin powder

1 cup (250 mL) fresh blueberries, washed and cut in half

### Whipped Coconut Salt Cod

¼ cup (60 mL) kosher salt

2 medium Yukon Gold potatoes, scrubbed

½ pound (225 g) salt cod fillets, rinsed and soaked in
   fresh water for 24 hours

1 cup (250 mL) canned coconut milk

2 sprigs fresh thyme

1 whole clove garlic, peeled

1 bay leaf

¾ cup (175 mL) extra-virgin olive oil

2 teaspoons (10 mL) fresh lemon zest

1 teaspoon (5 mL) lemon juice

½ teaspoon (2 mL) white pepper

¼ teaspoon (1 mL) sea salt

**Make the Ackee Terrine** Brush the inside of an 8- × 4-inch (1.5 L) loaf pan with oil. Line it with plastic wrap, making sure to leave at least a 2 inches (5 cm) overhang on each side. This will help to easily pull the terrine out of the loaf pan once it's set.

Lay a few paper towels on a clean work surface. Arrange the ackee on the paper towels, allowing the towels to soak up any excess water.

Place the olive oil in a medium skillet over medium heat. Add the onion and 1 teaspoon (5 mL) of the thyme leaves. Cook until the onions are translucent, 7 to 9 minutes. Remove from the heat and set aside.

Place the water in a small saucepan over low heat. Add the gelatin and whisk to combine. Bring the mixture to a simmer. Let simmer for 5 minutes, stirring constantly. Remove the saucepan from the heat.

Place the ackee into a high-speed blender. Purée until creamy and smooth. With the blender running on low speed, slowly add the gelatin and water mixture to the ackee. Blend for an additional 1 minute, until combined. Transfer the ackee mixture to a large bowl. Fold in the blueberries, the onion mixture, and the remaining 1 teaspoon (5 mL) of thyme.

Transfer the mixture to the prepared loaf pan. Use a spatula to smooth the top of the terrine. Carefully fold the overhanging plastic wrap on top of the terrine. Place it in the fridge for at least 2 hours, or overnight, to set.

**Meanwhile, Make the Whipped Coconut Salt Cod** Preheat the oven to 350°F (180°C). Place the kosher salt in a mound on a baking sheet.

Place the whole potatoes onto the baking sheet on top of the salt mound. Bake for 45 minutes, until easily pierced with a fork. Let cool.

When the potatoes are cool enough to handle, cut them in half, lengthwise. Scoop the flesh from the skins, and mash using a food mill, ricer, or potato masher.

Drain the salt cod and place it in a medium saucepan. Cover with cold water and bring to a boil over high heat. Remove from the heat and drain. Return the cod to the saucepan. Add the coconut milk, thyme, garlic, and bay leaf. Set the saucepan over medium-high heat and bring to a simmer. Let simmer for 15 minutes. Remove the saucepan from the heat and let the cod stand in the cooking liquid for 20 minutes. Drain and discard the liquid, making sure to reserve the garlic. Discard the thyme and bay leaf.

Place the salt cod in the bowl of a stand mixer. Use a fork to flake the salt cod into small pieces, discarding any bones and silvery membranes. Fit the stand mixer with the paddle attachment and place the bowl on the stand. Turn the mixer on medium-high speed. Drizzle in the olive oil, mixing until fully incorporated. Add the mashed potatoes and lemon zest and juice, mixing just until incorporated. Add the pepper and sea salt. Mix until combined.

Remove the terrine from the fridge. Unfold the plastic wrap covering the top of the terrine. Grab hold of the plastic wrap overhanging the two long edges of the pan. Carefully lift the terrine from pan and place it on a clean cutting board. Run a knife under scalding water for about 30 seconds. This will help to achieve clean cuts. Cut the terrine into six 1¼-inch (3 cm) slices. Divide the slices among plates. If desired, use a kitchen torch to char the edges of the terrine, releasing the flavour and smell of ackee. Place a large spoonful of whipped coconut salt cod on top of each slice of terrine. Serve immediately.

# Banana Leaf Steamed Cod with Fish Tea *Serves 4*

*This is an homage to my father's fish-head soup and my mother's love of tea. Wrapping the fish in banana leaves protects it from the steam and intensifies the aromatics that build flavour in the dish. The tea, poured over the fish just before serving, brings in a more concentrated fish flavour. It is the same caramel colour as my mum's cup of Earl Grey—the one that I'd make for her whenever she asked me to. I love the ceremony of making tea, and this dish feels ceremonial.*

### Fish Tea

1 cup (250 mL) halved cherry tomatoes

½ bulb fennel, coarsely chopped

2 carrots, coarsely chopped

2 celery stalks, coarsely chopped

2 cloves garlic, smashed

2 tablespoons (30 mL) extra-virgin olive oil

1 teaspoon (5 mL) salt

1 pound (450 g) fresh fish bones and heads

4 sprigs of fresh thyme

4 scallions with ends trimmed, cut into thirds

2 allspice seeds

2 strips of orange peel, ½ inch (1 cm) wide

2 strips of lemon peel, ½ inch (1 cm) wide

10 cups (2.5 L) water

1 Earl Grey tea bag

1 cup (250 mL) cold salted butter, cubed

Salt and white pepper

### Banana Leaf Steamed Cod

1 package (16 ounces/500 g) frozen banana leaves, thawed

4 fillets (6 ounces/170 g each) of cod, or white fish
  of choice

1 tablespoon (15 mL) sea salt

1 teaspoon (5 mL) black pepper

8 lemon slices

12 sprigs of parsley *continued . . .*

4 sprigs of thyme

4 scallions with ends trimmed, cut in half

4 cups cooked jasmine rice, to serve

Preheat the oven to 375°F (190°C). Line a baking sheet with parchment paper.

**Make the Fish Tea** In a large bowl, place the tomatoes, fennel, carrots, celery, garlic, olive oil, and salt. Toss to combine. Spread the vegetables in an even layer on the prepared baking sheet. Roast for 15 minutes.

Place the fish bones and heads in a large saucepan. Add the thyme, scallions, allspice, orange and lemon peels, and roasted vegetables. Add the water. Bring to a boil over high heat. Reduce the heat to medium-low and simmer, uncovered, for 30 minutes.

Use a fine-mesh sieve to strain the stock. Discard the solids. Give the saucepan a quick rinse and return the stock to the saucepan. Place the Earl Grey tea bag in the hot stock and let steep for 1 minute. Remove the tea bag and discard.

Pour the stock into a blender, working in batches if necessary. Blend on medium speed, adding a few pieces of butter at a time. Continue blending until all of the butter is combined and the stock starts to thicken. If blending the stock in batches, makes sure to divide the amount of butter you add to each batch accordingly. For example, if you blend the stock in two batches, add half of the butter to the first batch and the remaining butter to the second batch. Add salt and white pepper, to taste. Set aside.

**Make the Banana Leaf Steamed Cod** Cut the banana leaves, crosswise, into eight 10-inch (25 cm) pieces. Carefully trim off the tough spine that runs along one edge of each leaf. Reserve the spines. Sprinkle the salt and pepper evenly over both sides of the cod fillets. Set side.

In a large dry skillet over high heat, or over open fire, heat the banana leaves one at a time for about 30 seconds on each side to soften them up and make them flexible. Once they start to heat up, the colour will change from light to dark green and the leaves will not crack if folded.

Place one of the cut banana leaves on a cutting board horizontally. Place a second banana leaf on top of the first vertically to form the shape of a cross. Place 2 lemon slices, 3 sprigs of parsley, 1 sprig of thyme, and 2 pieces of scallion in the centre of the banana leaves. Place one fish fillet on top of the scallions. Fold the four ends of the banana leaf over the fish to form a parcel. Wrap one of the reserved banana leaf ribs around the parcel and tie it tight to close, making sure none of the fish is visible. Repeat with the remaining fillets.

Fill a steamer pot about a third of the way up with water and bring to a boil over high heat. Place the banana leaf parcels in the steamer and steam, covered, for 15 minutes, making sure the water does not come into contact with the banana leaf. Remove the parcels from the steamer and let cool for 5 minutes. Meanwhile, reheat the fish tea for 3 minutes over low heat until it's nice and hot. Open the banana leaf to expose the fish, but do not remove the fish from the parcel.

Divide the fish tea among 4 teacups or ramekins. Place the fish in the banana leaf on each plate, alongside 1 cup (250 mL) of rice. Serve with the fish tea on the side. Pour the fish tea overtop of the fish and rice and enjoy.

# Peppa Shrimp
*Serves 4, as a starter*

*Picture clear plastic bags full of these bright-red prawns hanging from a vendor's stall. That's how Peppa Shrimp is served in Jamaica. Garlicky. Peppery. Smoky. It's a fiery street food that's best enjoyed with a cold Red Stripe beer. The natural sweetness of the plump prawns plays perfectly against the spicy Scotch bonnet peppers in the sauce. The recipe for quick pickle Scotch bonnets will yield more peppers than you need for this recipe. You can slice up the leftovers and use them to garnish just about any dish to which you want to add a little extra heat and acid. I love adding them to soups and sandwiches. If you can't find shrimp with their heads on, simply use headless shrimp. This dish is native to Saint Elizabeth Parish, next to the Black River, my mother's birthplace.*

### Court Bouillon Poached Shrimp

4 cups (1 L) water

2 cups (500 mL) Chardonnay wine

1 cup (250 mL) freshly squeezed orange juice

2 celery stalks, coarsely chopped

2 large carrots, coarsely chopped

1 bulb fennel, coarsely chopped

1 orange, sliced

1 lemon, sliced

1 leek, coarsely chopped

1 bay leaf

1 sprig fresh tarragon

1 tablespoon (15 mL) salt

2 pounds (900 g) large fresh or thawed frozen shrimp, shell and heads on

### Quick Pickle Scotch Bonnet Peppers

½ pound (225 g) Scotch bonnet peppers (a variety of colours), stemmed

1 cup (250 mL) apple cider vinegar

1 cup (250 mL) water

1 tablespoon (15 mL) salt

1 tablespoon (15 mL) pure liquid honey

**Peppa Sauce**

1 Quick Pickle Scotch Bonnet Pepper

2 cups (500 mL) court bouillon poaching liquid

2 tablespoons (30 mL) quick pickle Scotch bonnet peppers liquid

8 cloves garlic

½ cup smoked paprika

2 tablespoons (30 mL) onion powder

¼ cup (60 mL) fresh lemon juice

¼ cup (60 mL) fresh orange juice

¼ cup (60 mL) fresh lime juice

1 teaspoon (5 mL) celery salt

**For Garnish**

½ cup (125 mL) chopped fresh parsley

¼ cup (60 mL) chopped scallions, green parts only

**Make the Court Bouillon Poached Shrimp** Place the water in a large saucepan over high heat. Add the Chardonnay, orange juice, celery, carrots, fennel, orange and lemon slices, leek, bay leaf, tarragon, and salt. Bring to a boil. Reduce the heat to medium-low and let simmer for 20 minutes. Fill a large bowl with ice water.

Add the shrimp to the court bouillon and poach the shrimp for 5 to 9 minutes, or until the shrimp turn pink. Using a slotted spoon, remove the prawns from the saucepan and place them directly in the ice bath. Reserve the poaching liquid.

**Make the Quick Pickle Scotch Bonnet Peppers** Place the Scotch bonnets in a medium heatproof bowl.

In a small saucepan over medium-high heat, place the vinegar, water, salt, and honey. Bring to a boil. Pour the liquid over the Scotch bonnets. Let cool to room temperature. Store leftover peppers in an airtight container in the fridge in the pickling liquid for up to 30 days.

**Make the Peppa Sauce** In the jar of a blender, place the quick pickle Scotch bonnet pepper, court bouillon poaching liquid, quick pickle liquid, garlic, paprika, onion powder, lemon, orange, and lime juice, and celery salt. Blend until you have a smooth, rich red sauce.

Remove the prawns from the ice bath and place them in a medium bowl. Use paper towels to pat off any excess water. Add the peppa sauce to the bowl with the prawns. Toss until all of the prawns are evenly coated.

Divide the Peppa Shrimp evenly among four plates. Garnish with the parsley and scallions. Enjoy—and be sure to suck the heads. They're the best part!

# Oxtail Patties  *Makes 12 patties*

*When I was ten, my dad wanted to open a shop selling Jamaican patties. He found a possible location that had a drop ceiling and a stained beige carpet. He wanted the countertop to face the door so he could welcome customers who might come in for a quick bite and stay for a domino match out back with the old-timers. His dream didn't happen, but at home on the occasional Sunday afternoon, we made patties anyway. We rolled out the dough and filled it with ground beef, lightly seasoned with diced onions and minced garlic. I watched Daddy use the tines of the fork to make indentations on the edges of the half-moon buttered pastries. They were stuffed full to bursting. Patties represent the gateway to Jamaican food—the comforting, flaky crust with its richness in colour and texture represents the spirit of the people of our motherland.*

*Cooking the oxtail filling takes 4 to 5 hours, so you may want to plan to spread the preparation for this dish over two days, making the filling on the first day and preparing the patty dough and making the patties on the second day.*

### Oxtail Filling

2 tablespoons + 2 teaspoons (40 mL) extra-virgin olive oil, divided

3 pounds (1.35 kg) whole beef oxtail

1 tablespoon + 1 teaspoon (20 mL) salt, divided

2 teaspoons (10 mL) black pepper, divided

3 cups (750 mL) finely chopped yellow onion, divided

3 cloves garlic, minced, divided

4 scallions with ends trimmed, coarsely chopped

6 cups (1.5 L) water

1 can (24 ounces/700 mL) tomato purée

2 tablespoons (30 mL) fresh thyme leaves

½ teaspoon (2 mL) ground allspice

1½ teaspoons (7 mL) Worcestershire sauce

1 red Scotch bonnet pepper, seeded and coarsely chopped

### Patty Dough

4 cups (1 L) all-purpose flour

1 cup (250 mL) cold unsalted butter, cubed

1 tablespoon + 2 teaspoons (25 mL) turmeric, divided

1 tablespoon (15 mL) granulated sugar

*continued . . .*

1 teaspoon (5 mL) kosher salt

1 cup (250 mL) ice water

2 large eggs

Preheat the oven to 375°F (190°C).

**Make the Oxtail Filling** Place 2 teaspoons (10 mL) of the olive oil in a large skillet over medium-high heat. Add the oxtail and sear for 5 minutes on each side, until browned. Transfer the oxtail to a roasting pan and season with 1 tablespoon (15 mL) of the salt and 1½ teaspoons (7 mL) of the pepper. Add 1 cup (250 mL) of the onion, one-third of the garlic, and 2 of the scallions. Cover with the water and tomato purée. Stir to combine. Cover with foil. Roast in the oven for 4 to 5 hours, until completely cooked and the meat is beginning to fall off the bone. Let cool.

When the oxtail is cool enough to handle, remove the meat from the bone and place it in a medium bowl. Pour any juices remaining in the roasting pan on top.

In a large skillet over high heat, place the remaining 2 tablespoons (30 mL) olive oil. Add the remaining 2 cups (500 mL) onion and cook until translucent, about 3 minutes. Reduce the heat to medium and add the remaining garlic, the thyme, the remaining ½ teaspoon (2 mL) pepper, and the allspice. Continue to cook for about 3 minutes, stirring occasionally. Add the pulled oxtail, the remaining scallions, the Worcestershire sauce, and the Scotch bonnet. Stir and cook for an additional 7 minutes, until the meat is warmed through and the mixture is well seasoned. Let cool.

**Make the Patty Dough** In a stand mixer fitted with the paddle attachment, add the flour, butter, 1½ tablespoons (22 mL) of the turmeric, the sugar, and the salt. Mix on low speed until the mixture is the texture of breadcrumbs. With the mixer still running on low speed, slowly add the ice water and mix until combined. The dough should come together to form a ball. If you do not have a stand mixer, you can make dough by hand: in a bowl, combine the flour, butter, 1½ tablespoons (22 mL) of the turmeric, the sugar, and the salt. Add the butter and work through until well combined, about 5 minutes.

Turn the dough out onto a clean cutting board and wrap it tightly in plastic wrap. Refrigerate for 30 minutes.

Preheat the oven to 350°F (180°C). Line two baking sheets with parchment paper.

**Assemble the Oxtail Patties** Cut the patty dough into 12 equal pieces and use your hands to roll each one into a ball. Dust a clean work surface like a countertop or a cutting board with some flour. Roll out one ball of dough at a time into a circle 4 to 6 inches (10 to 15 cm) in diameter. Arrange the dough rounds on the prepared baking sheets.

In a small bowl, whisk the eggs, the remaining ½ teaspoon (2 mL) of turmeric, and 1 teaspoon (5 mL) of water. Divide the oxtail filling equally among the dough rounds (about ⅓ cup/75 mL each), placing it in the middle. Brush the edges of the dough with the egg mixture. Fold each round in half over the filling to create a half-moon shape. Use a fork to press down on the edges and seal each patty, dipping the fork in a bit of flour as you go along the edges of the patty. Brush the tops of each patty with the remaining egg mixture.

Bake for 20 minutes, until golden brown. Let cool for 5 minutes, and enjoy!

# 100K Curry Chicken *Serves 4*

*Where's the vinegar? I'm in the poultry demo at the Natural Gourmet Institute, and I'm looking for the vinegar. The instructor is just patting the chicken dry and then nothing, no washing. What is this? Reports say that washing your chicken can cause bacteria to spread to kitchen surfaces and utensils. That will never stop Black folks from doing what feels right. In my childhood kitchen in Plantation, my mum would douse the chicken in vinegar for each and every dish. Roast chicken. Chicken in a bag. Curry chicken. My mum used store-bought curry spice for her curry chicken. I wanted to create my own spice blend and put my own stamp on this dish. It seemed to work! This is the dish that my angel investor fell in love with, and with his gift, Johnnie and I were able to open Saturday Dinette.*

### Curry Spice Mix

1 tablespoon (15 mL) coriander seeds

1 tablespoon (15 mL) cumin seeds

2 teaspoons (10 mL) whole allspice

2 teaspoons (10 mL) yellow mustard seeds

2 teaspoons (10 mL) fenugreek seeds

1½ teaspoons (7 mL) black peppercorns

1 whole dried clove

2½ tablespoons (37 mL) turmeric

2 teaspoons (10 mL) ground ginger

1 teaspoon (5 mL) ground nutmeg

1 teaspoon (5 mL) ground cinnamon

½ teaspoon (2 mL) cayenne pepper

### Curry Chicken

3 pounds (1.35 kg) chicken quarters

½ cup (125 mL) curry spice mix

4 cloves garlic, smashed

1 large yellow onion, diced

2 teaspoons (10 mL) extra-virgin olive oil

2 tablespoons (30 mL) kosher salt

1 tablespoon (15 mL) canola oil

3 cups (750 mL) chicken stock

*continued . . .*

2 bay leaves

1 whole Scotch bonnet pepper, any colour

4 Yukon Gold potatoes, peeled and diced

2 cups (500 mL) canned coconut milk

Salt and pepper

2 cups (500 mL) steamed white basmati rice, to serve

**For Garnish** (optional)

1 cup (250 mL) toasted cashews

½ cup (125 mL) toasted unsweetened coconut flakes

Fresh cilantro leaves and stems

Mango chutney

**Make the Curry Spice Mix** In a medium dry skillet over high heat, toast the coriander, cumin, allspice, mustard, fenugreek, peppercorns, and clove for 2 to 4 minutes, until fragrant. Remove from the heat and let cool for 2 minutes. Transfer the spice mix to a spice grinder, mortar and pestle, or to a high-speed blender. Grind to a powder. Transfer the powder to a small bowl. Add the turmeric, ginger, nutmeg, cinnamon, and cayenne. Stir to combine. Set aside.

**Make the Curry Chicken** Trim off any excess fat from the chicken. Cut each chicken quarter into 3 equal pieces and place them in a large bowl. (Using a serrated knife can be helpful for this, particularly on the skin.) Add the curry spice mix, garlic, onion, olive oil, and salt. Use your hands to massage the mixture into the chicken pieces until they are evenly coated. Cover the bowl with plastic wrap and place the chicken in the fridge to marinate for at least 4 hours, or overnight.

Remove the chicken from the fridge. Place the canola oil in a large saucepan over medium-high heat. Add enough of the chicken (and the onions and garlic) to cover the bottom of the pot. Cook until the chicken is browned on all sides, 5 to 7 minutes. Transfer the chicken to a clean bowl. Repeat until all of the chicken has been browned.

In the same saucepan you used to brown the chicken, add the chicken stock, bay leaves, Scotch bonnet, and chicken pieces. Bring to a boil over high heat. Reduce the heat to low and let simmer, uncovered, for at least 35 minutes, or until the chicken is completely cooked and beginning to fall off the bone.

While the curry is simmering, place the potatoes in a medium stock pot. Fill the pot with water to cover the potatoes by at least 2 inches. Place the pot over high heat and bring to a boil. Reduce the heat to low and let simmer for 15 minutes, until tender. Drain.

Add the coconut milk to the saucepan with the chicken and stir to combine. Let simmer for an additional 10 minutes. Add the potatoes. Stir to combine. Add salt and pepper to taste.

**Toast the Cashews** Preheat a medium skillet over medium-high heat. Add the cashews and give the skillet a shake to ensure they're arranged in a single layer. Toast for 3 to 5 minutes, stirring constantly, until the nuts are golden brown and fragrant. Immediately transfer the nuts to a medium bowl to cool.

Just before serving, remove the bay leaves and the Scotch bonnet from the curry chicken and discard. To serve, place ½ cup (125 mL) steamed rice in each bowl. Ladle the curry overtop. Garnish each serving with some toasted cashews, toasted coconut, fresh cilantro, and mango chutney, if desired.

# Nicey's Dutch Apple Pie _Makes 1 pie_

_My mum's strong hands on top of mine. I'm eight years old, and she's showing me how to press a mixture of flour and butter onto warm apples. I can smell cinnamon and nutmeg. Feel the soft skin of her inner arm against mine as the indentations of my fingers appear on the crust. It's a beautiful memory of our kitchen on a Sunday afternoon. Sunday night dinner always included dessert when I was a kid, and this was one of my favourites. Mum always used the store-bought graham cracker shells. She was a working mum, six days a week. Office job. Then cleaning offices. Then cleaning and cooking at home. Our mothers, bless them, truly. This recipe takes me right back home._

_I made my mum's apple pie when I first met Suzanne Hancock, and it started this whole project. Got me thinking about Nicey, my journey, got Suzanne thinking about her own losses and how sharing them can be healing. I hadn't talked about my mum's death much before that, and it made me want to celebrate her life._

6 Granny Smith apples, peeled and cored

2 tablespoons (30 mL) granulated sugar

1 teaspoon (5 mL) orange zest

½ cup (125 mL) water

1½ cups (375 mL) salted butter

3 cups (750 mL) all-purpose flour, sifted

1 cup (250 mL) firmly packed brown sugar

2 teaspoons (10 mL) cinnamon

1 teaspoon (5 mL) ground nutmeg

½ teaspoon (2 mL) sea salt

Pinch of ground allspice

Store-bought 9-inch (23 cm) graham cracker pie shell

Vanilla ice cream, to serve

Preheat the oven to 350°F (180°C).

Cut the apples into half-moon-shaped slices, about ¼ inch (5 mm) thick, and place them in a medium saucepan. Add the granulated sugar and orange zest. Toss until the apples are evenly coated. Add the water and cover. Place the saucepan over medium-low heat and cook for about 8 minutes, until the apples start to soften, making sure they do not turn mushy.

In a small saucepan, melt the butter over medium-low heat. Continue to cook for about 12 minutes, until the butter browns slightly and begins to develop some flavour. Let cool for 1 minute.

In a medium bowl, add the flour, brown sugar, cinnamon, nutmeg, salt, and allspice. Stir to combine. Add the melted butter to the bowl with dry ingredients. Use a wooden spoon to stir until the mixture resembles the texture of coarse sand, with lumps of sugar, butter, and salt.

Transfer the apples and any liquid in the saucepan to the graham cracker pie shell and level off the top. Use your hands to pile the flour and butter mixture on top of the apples, patting the flour mixture down with each addition and making sure to round the top of the mound. Don't worry if it looks dry or it cracks.

Bake for 40 minutes, or until the top of the pie looks golden brown and you can see the apple filling bubbling on the edges. Let cool before serving each slice of pie with a scoop of vanilla ice cream.

# Black Cake  *Makes two 9- × 5-inch loaves*

*Grandma's hands knew the measurements. Dash of nutmeg. A little less allspice
and cloves. Orange. Lemon. Rum. Dried fruit. For some people, cooking is a feeling.
I don't think she even needed to write down the recipe. And Black Cake is all
about feeling. It celebrates marriages and holidays, and making it requires
patience. A full year (although you can make it after a day). But the darker
the berry, the sweeter the juice. After a wedding, Black Cake is given as
a thank-you, and guests take it home. It symbolizes the sweetness of the love
that was celebrated.*

### Rum-Soaked Dried Fruit

*(makes 10 cups, enough for 6 loaves)*

2 cups (500 mL) pitted prunes

2 cups (500 mL) dried currants

2 cups (500 mL) black raisins

2 cups (500 mL) dried apricots

2 cups (500 mL) dried cherries

Peel of 2 oranges, without the pith

4 cups (1 L) dark rum

1 vanilla bean sliced in half lengthwise

2 whole star anise

### Black Cake

3 cups (750 mL) rum-soaked dried fruit

2½ cups (625 mL) all-purpose flour

2 teaspoons (10 mL) baking powder

1½ teaspoons (7 mL) ground cinnamon

1 teaspoon (5 mL) kosher salt

½ teaspoon (2 mL) ground nutmeg

¼ teaspoon (1 mL) ground allspice

¼ teaspoon (1 mL) ground cloves

1 cup (250 mL) unsalted butter, softened

1 cup (250 mL) brown sugar

6 large eggs

Zest of one lemon

*continued . . .*

Zest of one orange

2 teaspoons (10 mL) pure vanilla extract

2 cups (500 mL) dark rum

### Nutmeg Whipped Cream

1 cup (250 mL) heavy cream

½ cup (125 mL) icing sugar

½ teaspoon (2 mL) freshly grated nutmeg

**Make the Rum-Soaked Dried Fruit** Place the prunes, currants, raisins, dried apricots, cherries, and orange peels in a large bowl. Toss to combine. Divide the fruit among two large glass jars with tight-fitting lids. Pour in the rum, dividing it evenly between the two jars. Add half of the vanilla bean and the star anise to each jar. Screw the lids on the jars and place them in a dark place in your kitchen. Let the dried fruit soak for at least 24 hours, or up to 1 year. You can use some now and leave the remaining fruit to soak until you want to make the recipe again.

Preheat the oven to 275°F (140°C). Line two 9- × 5-inch (2.5 L) loaf pans with parchment paper.

**Make the Black Cake** Open the jar of dried fruit. Add 3 cups (750 mL) of the soaked dried fruit to the bowl of a food processor, leaving the liquid in the jar with the remaining fruit. Fish out any star anise, orange peels, or vanilla pods that may have made their way into the food processor and return them to the jar to soak with any remaining fruit. Purée until smooth, making sure there are no lumps.

In a large bowl, sift the flour, baking powder, cinnamon, salt, nutmeg, allspice, and cloves. Whisk to combine.

In a stand mixer fitted with the paddle attachment, cream the butter and sugar on medium speed until fluffy and smooth. Reduce the speed to low. Add one egg at a time, mixing until incorporated. Add the lemon and orange zest and the vanilla extract. Mix until combined. Add the dried fruit purée ½ cup (125 mL) at a time, waiting until one addition is combined before adding the next. Add the flour mixture ½ cup (125 mL) at a time, waiting until one addition is combined before adding the next. Mix until fully incorporated.

Divide the batter evenly among the loaf pans. Bake for 1 hour. Poke a cake tester into the middle of the cake. If it doesn't come out clean, bake for an additional 10 minutes. Let cool in the pans for 15 minutes.

Place the rum in a medium bowl. Turn the loaves out onto a wire rack. Brush the rum onto the warm loaves. Let cool completely.

**Make the Nutmeg Whipped Cream** In the bowl of a stand mixer fitted with the whisk attachment, place the cream. Sift in the icing sugar. Whip to stiff peaks on medium-high speed, about 5 minutes. Remove the bowl from the stand and gently fold in the nutmeg.

Divide the Black Cake among plates and serve with a generous dollop of nutmeg whipped cream on top.

# ACKNOWLEDGEMENTS

**Suzanne Barr**

Who do I want to thank?

Thank you, my love. Johnnie, our story has a new home, beginning with Nice, France. Your patience and your encouragement helped to push me to the finish line. Thank you! I love you so deeply. Our next journey is just beginning with Myles.

My precious baby boy Mylessy: Mummy is always supporting and watching. This book is for you to understand my beginnings and my many adventures.

My dearest Tanya. You are more than my sister. You are my best friend, my mentor, my role model, my protector. Thank you to Wayne. My heart fills with love knowing you withstood all the odds against you and prevailed to become an incredible man. Thank you to Headley for finding us. You completed our family. We welcomed the love and continued together.

Thank you to my grandmothers for your hands, sense of flavour, the right amount in a pinch, and for your love of Jamaican cooking. Thank you to Ivy, Hilgay, Nicole, Charmaine, Sonia, Vernal, Raymond, and the many family members, friends, and folks I shared this journey with. Your memories and stories helped to uncover the missing pieces and complete the stories I longed to know and appreciate. With all of your support and encouragement, walking this path never felt lonely or intimidating. It is with so much joy and happiness that I send this book out into the universe. These are the memories and moments from my life, my family, and my ancestors, and future dreams.

Amanda, thank you for the gift that would ultimately lead me down this path to becoming a chef.

To Maxine Waters for showing me the way forward as a Black woman, an advocate, and a dreamer.

Abel, thank you for showing me how to put *me* on a plate and share my truth through my food, family, memories, and traditions. Thank you, Lisa, for giving me my first kitchen job in New York City and for teaching me about service and how to dominate as a female force in the kitchen. Thank you to my angel investor, Ben, for believing that I could make my dream a reality.

To the teams of talented humans at Saturday Dinette, The Gladstone Hotel, Sand and Pearl, Avling Brewery, and True True Diner, your commitment and dedication will always motivate me. Thank you for trusting me to lead you in the kitchen. I appreciate you sharing that space and doing that dance!

Dearest Michael, thank you for walking into Saturday Dinette and allowing us to feed you. You changed our whole trajectory. We went from a little Dinette to part of a growing movement.

To Laura, Nicole, Sam, Kamoy and Olivia: your commitment to this project and your desire to bring this story to life is on each page. Thank you and congratulations! We did it!

To Miriam, Joshna, Charlotte, Kamoy, Sheena and SH: thank you for blessing these recipes with your Midas touch and coming along for the ride.

Thank you to Suzanne Hancock. With your bravery and belief in my story, we created this beautiful work together. Thank you for walking this path with me and for honouring the work.

**Suzanne Hancock**

Deep thanks to Suzanne Barr for making Nicey's apple pie with me all those years ago. It was the first delicious step on this journey.

This process has been a co-creation from the beginning. Suzanne and I spent hundreds of hours talking and writing. I'd listen to her stories and write them down. Then she'd write her stories and we'd combine them with the pieces that I'd written.

Telling one's story is the ultimate gift, and I feel incredibly grateful Suzanne trusted me to help tell hers.

Huge thanks to Nicole Winstanley for believing in this work from the beginning and for helping us make this dream a reality. Laura Dosky, thank you for being an outstanding editor. Your enthusiasm, skillful suggestions and hard work over the past two years have made this book sing.

Thanks to Suzanne Robertson for allowing us to use her gorgeous images.

Thanks to Colin McAdam for his limitless love, countless suggestions, and constant support. To Lola McAdam for her patience and her bright eyes.

# PHOTO CAPTIONS

# IDIOMS

Nah every crab hole get crab
*Things do not always turn out the way you expect them to*

When coconut fall from tree he can't fasten back
*Some happenings can't be changed or reversed*

One one coco full basket
*Success does not come suddenly, it takes time*

Tiddeh fi mi tomorra fi yuh
*Everyone will face problems or achieve*
*success in his or her own time*

Pepper bun hot but it good fi curry
*Harsh advice might be good for you*

New broom sweep clean, but owl broom noe dem cahna
*We should strive for a happy blend between the old and*
*the new, combining the freshness of the new with*
*the valuable experience of the old*

**SUZANNE BARR** is one of Canada's most respected chefs, with a flair for fresh comfort food and a passion for local community, food security, and advocacy for BIPOC and LGBTQ2+ communities. She was the owner of the popular Toronto restaurant Saturday Dinette, head chef of True True Diner, and is the founder of the Dinettes Program, which trains young, marginalized women in the kitchen. Suzanne lives in Florida with her husband and son.

**SUZANNE HANCOCK** is a writer, food-lover, and producer who lives on a mountain in Quebec.